The Best Canadian Poetry in English 2015

The Best Canadian Poetry in English 2015

Guest Editor · **Jacob McArthur Mooney**

Series Editor · **Molly Peacock**

Assistant Series Editor · **Anita Lahey**

TIGHTROPE BOOKS

The Canadian Copyright Licensing Agency:
www.accesscopyright.ca, info@accesscopyright.ca

Tightrope Books Inc.
2 College Street, Unit 206-207
Toronto, ON M5G 1K3
www.tightropebooks.com

Series Editor: Molly Peacock
Guest Editor: Jacob McArthur Mooney
Assistant Series Editor: Anita Lahey
Managing Editor: Heather Wood
Copy Editors: Brent Raycroft, Natalie Fuerth
Cover Design: Deanna Janovski
Cover Art: Kara Kosaka
Typesetting: Dawn Kresan

Canada Council
for the Arts

Conseil des Arts
du Canada

ONTARIO ARTS COUNCIL
CONSEIL DES ARTS DE L'ONTARIO
an Ontario government agency
un organisme du gouvernement de l'Ontario

Produced with the support of the Canada Council for the Arts and the Ontario Arts Council.

A cataloguing record for this publication is available from Library and Archives Canada. Printed in Canada.

CONTENTS

Foreword

Love, yes, plus its downside, loss: these are the only two subjects of poetry. They are the two reasons we in 21st-century Canada can bond immediately to an ancient voice when we read a verse that was at first chanted and then written down in hieroglyphics or ideograms or the alphabet of a dead language and translated later into our own. The intuitive connection between what we desire and the end of that desire is something the writers in this book all appreciate. They understand that poets from all time and everywhere have sought to put into words what we never thought could live in words. The ineffable? They seek to comprehend it. The work they set themselves? Simple: articulate the ineffable. That is the task of poetry.

Does this mean the fifty poets in this book, chosen by stellar guest editor Jacob McArthur Mooney, all sat down to write Huge Works on the Universal? Not at all. Poems live in their details. Each poet sits down to write quite specifically, out of a mind and circumstance that is the poet's alone, and each generation of poets speaks in its own language, with its own preoccupations. That is why those two subjects of poetry, love and death, morph and change and revivify and rise and make each poem afresh. And that is also why *The Best Canadian Poetry in English*, now in its eighth year, comes to you startlingly fresh each time.

We scour over fifty sources of poetry in Canada, from long-established print journals to pop-up online zines, to find just what ineffabilities—and inevitabilities—poets are putting into words right now. We encounter hundreds of poets—did you know Canada has *hundreds* of poets?—from prize-winning long-revered voices to those just emerging, and all to find you the best poems published within the past year that convey our deep concerns as a culture. Even though Canada is hardly monolithic, there really are things that concern every one of us, wherever we live, at whatever age, in whatever phase of life. Every one of us falls in love. Every one of us loses something or someone who meant a world, and now feel our world changed. This is what poets know, and they make you know. They can memorialize change—in funny, strange, outrageous and crystallizing ways.

Before you begin these fifty beauties, you'll see two essays—don't skip them! "The Secretly Optimistic Skeptic" is by our assistant series editor, Anita Lahey. She illuminates crucial issues that rise up among our 2015 poems with the critical mind and graceful prose of one of a handful of poets in the world, let alone Canada, who is also a journalist. Lahey starts with the downside, our responses to mass extinction, and works her way to how poets realistically affirm. Emotional realism—the refusal to sentimentalize—is a big reason why we feel our best picks have a chance of really lasting. Who knows? Maybe one of them will be the ancient voice with whom a 23rd-century citizen of earth might bond.

After Lahey's essay comes "The South-Facing Window," Jacob McArthur Mooney's explanation of his process of selecting poems for this year's volume. Mooney, the author of two exciting books of poetry, curator of a poetry reading series, reviewer of poetry, and our youngest guest editor so far, is not afraid of the difficult. The poets he's chosen—electric, moody, snappy, willing to leap among ideas and images, and also willing to direct their poems as spotlights into our intimate relations—make a landscape of our Canadian lives at this moment. *The Best Canadian Poetry 2015* stands for a paradox: just as our anthology takes the temperature of our times with current poems, it also gambles on poems we hope will stand the test of times to come.

After Mooney selected his longlist of 100 poems, Anita Lahey and I, who had also been reading along, began extended Skype conversations with him, during which we hashed out the list of the final fifty. We are proud to say that twenty-nine of Mooney's chosen poets are brand new to this anthology. At the end of this volume we also present a list of Notable Poems of 2014. Here we include poems by writers we hope you'll watch for in the future, and tip our hat to poets who have already been well-represented in our eight books so far. It's always tough to hammer out the poems to include, and we append this broader list to show the depth and variety across the country we have to choose from, and to point our readers to more. After all, if our poets set themselves the challenge of putting into words what has never been in words (and falls into those two age-old categories of human passion and grief), and if our eclectic literary journals both print and post them, we aim to celebrate as many successes as we can.

Molly Peacock
Toronto, ON

The Secretly Optimistic Skeptic

This year's collection of the best Canadian poems published in English opens with a gripping plea, John Wall Barger's "Urgent Message from the Captain of the Unicorn Hunters." Just about every sin humanity has enacted, reenacted and perpetuated throughout history is housed within the imagined world of this poem, in which unicorns have been demonized, tortured, enslaved, and hunted for their healing and aphrodisiac properties. Think any of a half dozen genocides. Think Abu Ghraib. Think seahorses and impotence, shark fins and cancer. Human trafficking, child prostitution. The "Captain," in a passionate shout of remorse, calls to a halt the greed, cruelty, racism, speciesism, superstition and plain old violence that have fueled what we, as readers, can intuit has been nothing less than a war on magic, beauty and myth—all those ineffable qualities truly embodied by unicorns—all those elements we need, not to live, but to live with any hope. Let the long-suffering unicorns "loose in their fields of sorrow," the captain commands, warning, ominously, that the unicorns' recourse, once set free, is out of his hands. "First, *let them go.* And then we wait."

We wait. These days, we wait upon an impressive range of apocalyptic fates that—like the unicorn hunters who so dutifully followed orders—we have by all accounts brought upon ourselves. We're well down the road toward devastating climate change, wholesale species extinction, and island countries vanishing under rising sea waters. Drinking water is due to dry up. Deserts are expanding. Civil war and terrorists proliferate. In supposedly defending ourselves against the latter, we meekly relinquish all manner of hard-won rights and freedoms. The most despairing among us might be wrong about where all of this leads. Human beings are instinctively braced for devastation, real or imagined. We can only operate on the evidence before us, passed through whatever concentration of perspective we're able to concoct. By these parameters, right now, from what we can see and comprehend, things have never looked so bad. As American author Jonathan Franzen writes in a piece called "Carbon Capture" that was published in the *New Yorker* on April 6, 2015—an essay every bit as urgent as Barger's poem—"drastic planetary overheating is a done deal." Though this is an introduction to a collection of poetry, and he may be the furthest thing from a poet in the world of writers, let's stick with Franzen for a moment. His question is whether it's OK, in the face of our current reality, to care about the fate of a particular species of bird. A warbler, say. Warblers are likely to die in the thousands if a glass-walled stadium is erected in New York City. If protecting that bird distracts us (and any resources and smarts we can muster) from the larger problem of climate change, are we wrong to do our best, nonetheless, to protect it? Franzen conducts a neat flip in moral compassing, calling our focus on climate change easy because it's a big, vague, everywhere problem: everyone's and therefore no-one's fault. He comes down on the side of the warblers, whose problem is more personal, for them, for him, and for the builders of the stadium: you can't help this bird without making actual, nameable people and organizations uncomfortable, and culpable. There's no dispersing this problem like so much leaked oil in the Gulf. Franzen writes, "We can dam every river and blight every landscape with biofuel agriculture, solar farms and wind turbines, to buy some extra years of moderated warming." Or, he proposes, each of us can choose to focus on "helping something you love, something right in front of you." Put another way: "The Earth as we now know it resembles a patient whose terminal cancer we can choose to treat either with disfiguring aggression or with palliation and sympathy."

I don't bring this up as a call to arms, but to underline that this is the context in which today's poets are composing. Every spring melt and rolling cloud bank brings threat of catastrophic flood. Each inching upward of the annual temperature corresponds with the cracking and vanishing of an ice shelf as vast and weighty as the landscape of your childhood; its every revelation, confusion, triumph and disappointment laid end-to-end and dashed into Antarctic waters. We're in the midst of an unprecedented mass extinction event. The lay of the land is bleak, so bleak that those tired old questions—*Why poetry? What is poetry good for?*—can't help but rear. Is it not the height of farce, when the whole show of existence is crashing down around you, to spend the morning at your desk seeking a reasonable rhyme for "spring peeper"? Stretching your legs, reheating your coffee in the microwave, glancing out the window at the rain, sitting down to get back at it?

Creeper. Sleeper. Deeper. Keep her.

*

O, the uncountable and impressive variety of ways in which we have failed and are failing our planet, and our very selves. An air of dismal recognition infects line after line of the poems in this year's Best Canadian Poetry anthology, thoughtfully and enthusiastically selected by guest editor Jacob McArthur Mooney. We have here poems as mea culpas, elegies, pleas for forgiveness, ironic (and revealing) twists in awareness, narratives of tragically preventable mistake, the straightforward beats of *God help us, look what we've done. This time. Again.* Bleak? Hell, yes. But also thrilling. Eye-opening. Funny (occasionally side-splitting). Dare I say it? I'll almost say it. Nearly, a little bit, barely a whiff: redemptive. These poems reveal our contemporary keepers of the craft pulling off a complex, gripping, often breathtaking dance of political and emotional sophistication. These are poems that mean, and poems that perform: poems that win the heart, the mind, the eye; the secretly optimistic skeptic within us all.

Where to start? In "Truth, power and the politics of Carbon Capture," Lesley Battler takes on the unappealing role of poetic conscience for the oil and gas industry, as well as for academia's potentially toxic habit of intellectualizing, in a poem that entangles the scathing cultural critiques of Michel Foucault with the government's weasel-like habit of discrediting environmental science and even individual experience. "Though activism didn't exactly / begin with the Silent Spring business I believe / that sordid affair provoked numerous questions / around Power and Knowledge." Julie Bruck's "Two Fish" is a piercing examination of the discomfort imposed by survivors on those responsible for their suffering. Which neglected fish, Bruck asks, is more chilling, the one "distorted / as in a funhouse mirror, one eye bulging," or the one that, inexplicably, lives? "The hideously damaged one, or the one / who moves on as if this was what it meant / to be entrusted to your care? Which fish?" Consider the teeth mailed to Washington by the mothers in Anne-Marie Todkill's "Strontium-90," a peace protest and attempt to prove "that death's particulates / have fallen" from test bombs, from human error, from an endless, ongoing history of poor decisions. Even one moment of failure, a single lapse, can reassert itself and claim some kind of reparation—or choose to refuse it. In Jonathan Bennett's "Palliative Care Reflective Portfolio," a dying physician accepts kindness from a social worker he once treated with disrespect, who now "intuits what / no one else can." Bennett writes, the line dripping with desperation, for the narrator's hour is close at hand and a clean conscience is the only thing left to secure: "I apologize to her all night."

There are no apologies in George Elliott Clarke's merciless recounting, through apparently reconstituted news report texts, of a group of slaves trapped in a burning house: "I had to navigate fluid meat" and "The dead were largely invisible under my boot-steps" and "The burnt-over area resembles gravestone shale / or a tar oasis." Nor are there any in Lucas Crawford's remarkable "Failed Séances for Rita MacNeil (1944-2013)," which, with an underlay of intimacy and wry humour, transforms the late MacNeil into a talisman for every marginalized person, and by extension, every misunderstood or underestimated or overlooked or wrongly judged living thing, past and present. Crawford declares, "Rita, we are both members of the fat neo-Scottish diaspora. / Don't tell me it doesn't exist, sweet darlin' / until you are the only fat transsexual / at a Rankin Family concert in Montreal." Crawford's elegy is raucous and raw, a twinning of fierce politics and honest emotion, rarely to be found in poetry or elsewhere. So, too, Karen Solie's elegy "For the Ski Jump at Canada Olympic Park, Calgary," which asks the obsolete ski jump to stand in for a lost, better humanity, one that may never have existed, one in which tourists on the observation platform might see more than "the accelerating ritual of supply / and demand." Solie's final, cold dismissal of the ski jump is surprisingly affecting, as if something living and breathing has been forsaken, because her metaphor is so well-wrought, her tone spot-on: "You've outlived your design. / Would need to be retrofitted for safety / and who has that kind of time."

Note the absence of a question mark.

It's nothing new to contend that poetry confronts what we would sometimes rather look away from, be it the unbearable ecstasies of love or the searing pain of grief—or the horrors caused by our very own actions and inactions. In his essay "Education by Poetry" Robert Frost makes an eloquent case for the necessity of what I'll call metaphoric literacy, because, he deftly illustrates, metaphor is embedded in the most innocent of exchanges, and also in the ways we review and consider everything from our behaviour to our very existence: "unless you are at home in metaphor, unless you have had your proper poetical education in the metaphor, you are not safe anywhere ... you are not safe with science, you are not safe in history." He describes how poetry begins in "trivial metaphors, pretty metaphors, 'grace' metaphors, and goes on to the profoundest thinking that we have." That is simply because, as Frost reminds us, "Poetry provides the one permissible way of saying one thing and meaning another." The beauty of metaphor, Frost contends, is in the fact that it eventually breaks down: metaphor can only take us so far. And we must be deeply intimate with its ways in order to know when we're approaching its limits. "You don't know how much you can get out of it, and when it will cease to yield. It is a very living thing. It is as life itself."

Metaphor is simultaneously our way out of, and back into, our own reality. It drops us back in with our vision punched into focus, having encountered words—the fittest words, tightly coiled and sparely employed—as fists. Writing and reading poetry is no escape, but a bracing procedure for facing-up, for taking it in the eye. For being shaken loose and righting ourselves, and through that dust-up, blessedly, if briefly, "being" in a way that is more whole, more solid, than our usual mode of being.

Now, I'm not suggesting that recording our sins and failings in winning rhythms, filtered cleverly through metaphor, wipes them away. However persistently the two have been equated over time, poetry is not the confessional. Indeed, I would propose that what we're dealing with here are post-confessional poems. Poems that see your admission of guilt and raise you one conflicting yet utterly true moment of wonder; that see your shame and raise you a two-step of deep, still observation; that see your determined witnessing of atrocity and raise you a counter-quartet of alchemic linguistic layering. We have heard this before, and known it before, and every poet who sits down to write, every reader who confronts a lined text, is in some aspect of her being remembering: poetry is a way through. Not *the* way through, but one way. And it happens to be the way that's equipped to consider and weigh, illustrate and enact, the nature and efficacy of all possible alternatives.

Make no mistake. There's joy in these poems, huddled in the midst of their catastrophic subject matter, bubbling through their remorse and their regret, their rising panic, their "How will we ever fix this mess?" There's joy in their making, and in the many ways they infiltrate and shake up the atmosphere while being read. Especially aloud. Try them aloud. Hear that last line of Elena Johnson's "I Don't Bother Canning Peaches" clunk down with its self-deprecating loss of faith embedded neatly (and sadly) in faith's stubborn declaration: "Food will drop from the sky." Hear the plea of Kasia Juno's Yeti crab, from the dark depths of Lake Vostok, as this heretofore undisturbed creature prepares to contend with the invasions of science: "We're not ready for the age of air / of polar wind / and sunshine." Recite A.F. Moritz's "Entrances," follow that voice into "the chasms of / minor darkness," and into "the space in earth the shape of the absence…" Let your voice ring out as the mother in Hoa Nyugen's "A Thousand Times You Lose Your Treasure" first mistakes the munitions for fireworks, then, a scant few lines later, prepares to disown her baby. Hum along with the discomfort, boredom, and fear (read: rising sense of mortality) that pervades Brenda Schmidt's "A Citizen Scientist's Life Cycle." Bellow Bardia Sinaee's unsettling discovery: "The human heart, despite its plumbing / and catalogue of attachments, can't signal before it turns."

It is not that writing poetry will save us, or excuse us. It's that we will, we must, write poetry whether we can save ourselves or not. This might amount to consolation, end-stop. Or it might amount to other things, as well. A little hatchway, say, toward the place where awareness—of sorrow, of guilt, of the march of time and its consequences—expressed frankly and artfully, leads. In "St. John's Burns Down for the Umpteenth Time," James Langer writes, "The way forward is more solitary but clearly defined, / and our consent in its direction can't be otherwise."

*

In her blessedly plainspoken essay at the start of Carol Ann Duffy's recent collection, *The World's Wife*, Jeanette Winterson revisits a subject she dealt with in her memoir, *Why Be Happy When You Could be Normal?* That is, the value of poetry: what poetry can do for an ordinary person, on an ordinary day, in an ordinary life. In the memoir, her encounter with the poetry of T.S. Eliot at the local library rescues her from the despair of a mentally and emotionally straitjacketed upbringing, and even from the immediate crisis of being kicked out of home at age sixteen. "I had no one to help me, but the T.S. Eliot helped me." Henceforth, for Winterson, poetry serves as lifeline, window, blanket, door. Now, in relishing Duffy's verse, she speaks again of the poem's numerous uses and delights. It's an "ancient means of communication" that must be "an evolutionary necessity." It's a "shot of espresso—the fastest way to get a hit of mental and spiritual energy." It's a lie-detector, "a rope in a storm," the world's "longest-running workshop on how to love," and "the acid-scrub of cliché." It is many, many things, but at the bottom of all these possibilities lies the one that has given this ancient craft its longevity: "Poetry is pleasure."

Poetry is pleasure. These are the three words that begin Winterson's introduction, and it seems silly that she or I or anyone would feel the need to write them. And yet, because poetry bears so much responsibility for profundity, it's a truth that bears repeating. I recently had a conversation along these lines with a retired English professor. He told me that when, as a young man, he was choosing the direction of his studies, he veered from philosophy to literature precisely because the latter offered a pathway into all the same meaty matter, with the bonus of entertainment. And why shouldn't we dress up our existential struggles in a pleasing garb? Why shouldn't we relish this work of questioning and comprehending—and simply contending with—life? Poetry is pleasure. The statement is not so simple as it first appears. Poetry is pleasure in its parts and in its effects, in its line-dancing and in its hypnotic call-and-response, in its making and in its tasting, in the stuff it tackles and how. The pleasure that poetry embodies and affords can be not just a means, but an end in itself, a form of salvation, or something that briefly feels like salvation, which, indulged in often enough, can amount to much the same thing. You know those studies on how the more you smile the happier you feel? The pleasure of poetry works this way, even, or especially when, it's paired with the grimmest of realities.

One of humankind's most enduring crafts and impulses does not require my defense. I'll just say this. When we make our music amid the tumble and cry of impending doom we are carving out our own wilderness protection zone, a place where rhythms and rhymes and undiscovered metaphors may thrive, and the same principal that Franzen outlines with regards to discrete ecosystems applies here too. If we do, after all, find our way through this uncommonly complex and sticky web of threats to life on Earth, it would sure help to come out the other side, twisted and bloody as we'll surely be, with our poetic ecology intact. That means our stomp and beat, our lingo and lift, our intellectual and emotional discourse, our compulsive human conversation dissected, sculpted, scanned, recited, chanted, mined. Poetry needs its healthy habitat as much as any warbler or grebe. For those of us who read it (and write it), poetry is that "something we love, something right in front of us," that we will put our all into protecting, because it is in our nature to do so. If we deny our nature, why would we care what happens to its home?

We offer you this "way forward." Venture into these woods. Follow this trail of letters. Read the undergrowth and dappled light within. Who knows, by the time you reach the clearing, what may have rooted, sprouted, bloomed, begun to flirt with decay. Where the freed unicorns will be, or the gist of their intent.

The South-Facing Window:
An Introduction to *The Best Canadian Poetry in English, 2015*

For several years, the poetry reading series I curate in Toronto's west end ran biweekly out of a bar the approximate size of a one-bedroom apartment. The bar fronted on Dundas West, probably the least romantic and strictly functional of the downtown's major streets. Dundas breaks Toronto's military grid by winding a bit; I once overheard a tour guide say it actually matches the city's original shoreline from when the Europeans first found it and took it for their own. Even though Lake Ontario now sits about a mile and a half to the south, we liked to think of the old venue as lakefront property.

I'm proud of the series, of the small claim to culture it's carved out for itself and its regular listeners. The old stage's best feature was a large picture window facing south towards the former shoreline. I find myself missing the view. I had gotten used to watching poets and authors read their work framed by the passing TTC vehicles, spelunking club kids, and slouch-shouldered locals. The whole city and the country beyond us.

The picture window played host to a kind of public theatre I had grown to love. It was possible to pay adequate attention to the readers while also spying walkers as they crossed our line of sight and evaluated. These wary visitors would pause in front of the picture window, glance down at the sandwich board advertising poems, look up, glance nervously at their friends or the door. Sometimes they'd spot the standing-room audience, stride blindly past the sandwich board, and find themselves a foot and a half away from a reader mid-way through some elegy or joke. Silence and focused listening all around them. They'd idle at the door, avoiding eye contact, eventually staying out of politeness or the power of our charm. Or they'd escape back out through the front door and stand in the clear gaze of the window, puzzled.

The window became the central articulation point between what I've come to understand as *my* world and *the* world: between my friends with our shared eccentricities and the rest of Canada. On one side of the picture window, poetry struggled to be known as something more than a historical curiosity or a collection of logic puzzles aimed at students. On our side of the window, it was the central organizing problem of modern life. Few borders are more pronounced.

The picture window as border has proven to be a sticky idea for me, and I feel it is a suitable starting image for this anthology, which has a tradition—unlike much poetry and certain poetry anthologies—of being read by non-poets as well as poets. The *Best Canadian Poetry in English* series stands at the same frontier as the window. It is made by those on our side as a kind of yearbook, summarizing and specifying changes in our culture, holding new voices up against the established. But, unlike a yearbook, it plugs into a broader access and is read by those on the other side of the window, too, those whose interest in poetry is more transient. For people who spend great amounts of their time, as I do, trying to coax people through the door and into the poetry-centric side of the glass, the lead concerns I bring to the task of guest editing this year's version are: What is welcoming, exactly? What opens that door and keeps it open?

Much energy has been spent trying to make poetry more welcoming, and much of the terrible poetry of the last, say, two generations has been published to an ethic of accessibility and ease-of-use. I am happy to report that there are no Accessible Poems in this anthology. There are as many as fifty welcoming poems, I think, but the poems' paths to being welcoming have been cleared more honestly and by more sophisticated tactics than by simply flattening their vocabulary or dumbing-down their ideas. I think (and this is an ethic I've tried to maintain both as the host of a reading series and as the guest editor of this anthology) that a key to presenting a welcoming docket of poems is to remain as variable in your picks as possible. But even this is fraught. There exists a kind of absolutism that can sneak up on inclusiveness, one that sheds the benefits of curation like it's some trap, and frankly I've worked too hard to carry that belief to its extreme. What I have done is try to include poems that are difficult, but in a variety of ways. Difficult, in the end, is reader-loving. Accessible, in the end, is a restraint. I have a great deal of faith in anyone who has crossed the great ocean of legal entertainments and picked this specific book out of the crowd, and I want very deeply to repay that unusual trust. An accessible poem is just an advertisement for a poem, while a good difficult one is a proof, a demonstration of the wildness available within the domesticated urges of our language.

The good ones can pose all kinds of questions, and elect to answer only a subset, while still leaving us satisfied on the exit. Within the anthology, I'd like to think that the wild Wikipedia-divers like Matt Rader's "SN1987AZT" and Brecken Hancock's "Evil Brecken" help express that specific wish the clearest. On the other hand, a good, hard, poem can present itself as almost too self-contained, too solved to be serious, and the riddle-inspired pieces like Julie Bruck's "Two Fish" and Troy Jollimore's "Some Men" stick in the brain as totems of a kind of apparent finished-ness that doesn't quite square with how much they keep moving in the brain after reading. There are difficult poems that arrive breathless with ambition (Lucas Crawford's tragicomic elegy; George Elliott Clarke's blazing historiographical account). There are difficult poems that politely hand you only half of their selves and withhold the rest for a lonely moment, like Elena Johnson's "I Don't Bother Canning Peaches" with its confident civic escapists. There are poems that use the structural possibilities of a poem for leverage, as with Amanda Jernigan's heavily enjambed mythic stitchback or Alexandra Oliver's subtle rhyme. And of course there are the poems that are so note-perfect, so polished and complete, that the difficulty comes from trying to imagine them as human-built creations, as former works-in-progress. I'm thinking here of Richard Greene's loving remembrance of the late poet Kildare Dobbs, or Brenda Schmidt's novelistic sonnet sequence.

But such examples won't get us to an accounting of all fifty poems in the book, and it's the in-between pieces that might be as close as I can take you to a sense of my own aesthetic (read: biases) as a reader and editor. I would propose that both Leah Horlick's "The Tower" and Susan Elmslie's "Gift Horse" are welcoming, difficult poems. Surely they are readable and friendly. In the picture window metaphor, they are the ones pressed up against the glass, waving in the walkers-by. Their difficulty lies in knowing all you can about them, while their welcoming makes that an exquisite form of recreation. If we say that the product of a great poem is the adoption of disparate or even opposite simultaneous reactions in the head of a reader, if you come to experience joy and shame or umbrage and optimism all at once, if you come to understand the window as both fronting and not fronting on the lake, then this may be the most difficult and transcendent game poetry can play, and it's one that Elmslie and Horlick (and Cara-Lyn Morgan, and Barry Dempster, and many others) have done with simple grace in these pages. I've tried to include, and in this I've been helped dramatically by series editors Molly Peacock and Anita Lahey, as many different kinds of difficulty as I can, to bring in poets who play against and even confront one another on aesthetics, politics, and place.

Another energy waste in recent years, to my eye as a citizen of the picture window's north side, has been the denouement of Canadian literature's fifty-year attempt at defining Canadianness for Canadians. This is the great public works project of post-war Canadian poetry, and many of the best books we've produced have been written to its edict. I would argue that returns, however, are dwindling. Decades on, I don't know if the poets ever came up with a conception of Canadianness that felt right for more than an archaic racial and political centre. Maybe they were never going to get there, and the best we could have hoped for were a few good books. We got our good books (Lee's *Civil Elegies*, Atwood's *The Journals of Susanna Moodie*, McKay's *Birding, or desire*, and others) but ended up with a new problem of "Canadianness" as genre: a kind of practiced, searchful, easily-awed poetry that, stripped of the political urgency of its birth, haunts us like bad maxims, forever offering easy ways out of lines and ideas using the well-trod paths of past generations.

There are poets who still find wonder in these corners, but for my dollar most of the great work is being done in a post-Canadian moment. By post-Canadian, I want to dismiss not national themes but rather national mechanics, an idea of poetry and place that treats the nation, its environment and people, as some kind of perfectible vessel made whole by myth and wisdom. As antidote, Lesley Battler's found dialogue is unrecognizable to the ecopoetry from our little magazines of the seventies. Likewise, Jeff Blackman's brief graffiti has the benefit of its nihilism: his speaker doesn't really have an alternate Canada to suggest, and so he snipes cathartically at the culture presented. The Disco Nationalists would have hated him. As counterpoint, Shane Neilson's poem is awash in Canadiana but is all the stronger for its refusal to escape through the emergency hatches offered by the last fifty years of Canadian lyric. From now on, if we are going to present the varied metaphor-machines of our urban spaces, let us do so with Lise Gaston's protest chants in our ears. If we are going to raid the newspapers for content, let it not just be the *Globe and Mail* but *The New York Times*, *The Guardian*, and whatever else Amber McMillan dug through for "Listen, Junebug." If we are to be crushed by the weight of our inherited canons, let us understand, as Robert Currie does, that this would at least be a whimsical death. Let's have our embossed national animal be John Wall Barger's unicorn. Let's have our work songs ding with Sadie McCarney's cash register, and if we, as Jan Zwicky did, come across an abandoned grain elevator set against a prairie sky, let's be both taken by its beauty and mad at its condition. Let's embrace our disparate reactions. Let's be patriotic post-Canadians together.

There are things I hope our late-night passers-by didn't think we got up to on our side of the window: accessibility, social studies, nation-building, and the like. But I don't control that. I spend so much time thinking about how they presented to us inside the bar that I keep forgetting about the fact that the mirror goes both ways: we are, for them, a kind of theatre too. We can be the stage for all their assumptions and uncertainties about poetry, about Canadian art, about art itself. Borders act on all of us.

Another good border zone is the Canadian Poetry section of our country's chain bookstores. Of course, as a steadfast member of the literati, I buy all my books at Indies and carry them home in hand-stitched wicker baskets, but I am often responsible for an infant who needs his diaper changed when on long walks, so the neighbourhood Indigo has become a regular stop. The big box stores have the arbitrariness of scale; they aren't assembled lovingly by a knowing hand and are instead the product of shipping patterns and stock overruns. In their own blunt way, they are a public. I like to go find their short Canadian poetry shelves, look on the bright neon covers (now suddenly as common as plaid in CanLit book design), and try to guess what I might pick up and leaf through if I didn't know anything about the authors. Most often, I find myself swayed by the implied curatorial safety of the anthology, and the big stores tend to have a *Best Canadian Poetry in English* of at least a somewhat recent vintage. I tell you this story as a way to express why I think this anthology is important.

Maybe you are reading these words right now in the Canadian poetry grotto of a Chapters or a Coles, considering where to spend your Art Dollar. I wonder how many of these poems you, individual reader, will like. What's a good number? Surely if you read through the book and say "All fifty" I'll know you're either lying or I've failed to make an adequately varied, adequately conflicted contribution as guest editor. But if you read them and say "None", I won't believe you either. Maybe your early opinion of the volume will reflect which poem you first flipped to. Will it be Jonathan Bennett's vocally distinct dramatic monologue? Kayla Czaga's slow turn to sweetness? Any of the poems that concern early parenthood? There are a lot of those, and while this can be read as a symptom of my own early parenthood, I would argue that the trend exists beyond this book, and beyond this country. Parents are spilling out into magazines, clutching poems. They have new ironies and joys and the worst, most unspeakable terrors. It's important to present all these propositions close to one another to allow for easy movement between them. You will like a certain fraction of these poems and, if we're all very lucky, hate a certain fraction of them, too.

The owner of the bar with the south-facing window has sold it, and it will now close for renovation. So, I am in the middle of a venue search, the first for the reading series since we opened seven years ago. This has sent me out the door, down the street, and into the vast unconcerned country to try and describe to bar and restaurant owners what exactly a reading series is and why they might want to house one. Thrown into Lake Ontario and told to swim. This is a rare practical test for my ideas about being welcoming. It is a challenge not just to consider the picture window, but to try and construct a new one. Luckily, I feel ready for the coming rebuild in large part because of my time spent guest editing this anthology. *Best Canadian Poetry in English* was also a practical test of these ideas, a way to solidify an ethic and fess up to my own bullshit. I would like to thank Molly Peacock and Anita Lahey for reading alongside me, Heather Wood and Jim Nason for keeping the machine running at Tightrope, and the several hundred poets we read this year. Not only the ones who made the anthology or the longlist, but all of them: for suffering my biases, my misreadings, and my curatorial agendas, none of which mattered at all to their writing or the accomplishment of their publication. This anthology is a real gift to a guest editor, and I'm happy to have learned so much about my peers.

I hope you find a topography in these pages: something to love, something to consider, something to be taken in by and either embrace or throw back. I want you to see how beautiful and various the view is from the north side of the window, looking out onto the world, the micro and the macro, the streetcar stop, the lake. So please, come inside. There are lights on in every corner.

The Best Canadian Poetry in English 2015

Urgent Message from the Captain of the Unicorn Hunters

Release them. Those sealed in your attics.
Those chained in your barns. Those on the nightmare yokes.
Those heads on your walls. This was our fault.
We taught you to torture the unicorn.
That it biteth like a lion & kicketh like a horse.
That it has no fear of iron weapons.
That unicorn-leather boots ensure sound legs
& protection from plague. That unicorn liver (with a paste
of egg yolk) heals leprosy. That its tusk,
ground to dust, gives a hard-on. Forget all that.
Ye taxidermists, cut out your work.
Keep off, ye farmers of dreams & horns.
We have done enough. Baiting them with our virgins.
Cutting the heads off the calves & their mothers.
Planting birthday candles in their eyes.
Fortune-telling with their gizzards.
Tossing their balls to the dogs.—Enough!
Free them, to bathe in our rainbows.
Let them loose in their fields of sorrow.
Enough have they tholed. And you'll have to forgive:
nothing that's happened as yet
has prepared me for this. I have taken us too far
off course. Abominations, treason!
It's up to them now, our lot.
First, *let them go.* And then we wait.

from *Prairie Fire*

Truth, power and the politics of Carbon Capture

Dialogue between OilWeek *and Michel Foucault sponsored by the Canadian government*

1.

It was open season on oil and gas when
landowners Jane and Justin Conn and the
activist group, EcoJustice, went public
with allegations CO_2 was leaking from
the underground reservoir.
    **No one knew the real problem
was environmental science and the ideological
functions it could serve.**
    They targeted both Cenovus
and the academics associated with the Weyburn-
Midale Carbon Capture and Storage Project.
    **Though activism didn't exactly
begin with the Silent Spring business I believe
that sordid affair provoked numerous questions
around Power and Knowledge.**

2.

Instead of looking at data that discredited
their claims the Conn gang ramped up the
rhetoric.
    **Their statements are verified by the
"media" of opinion, a materiality caught in
the mechanisms of power formed by the
press, cinema, TV, social networks.**

Before industry could respond, a rogue's gallery of faux scientists and axe-grinding activists arrived on site, blatting soundbites such as "We are here today on the frontier of climate destruction."

No one considered the interweaving of power and knowledge in a science as dubious as ecology riddled with ready-made concepts, approved terms of vocabulary.

Environmentalist show-trials make it appear the Canadian Energy Industry is the one committing criminal acts.

An entire discourse has risen from a population composed of people who "choose" to reduce, recycle and reuse according to precisely determined norms.

3.

According to Canadian Press dead animals were regularly found in a pit metres from the Conns' nuptial bed.

Activist dialectic evades the reality of spurious environmental science—enviromancy—by reducing it to a Hegelian skeleton.

Multicoloured scum bubbled in once bucolic ponds. "At night." Conn said, "We could hear this sort of cannon going off."

Semiology examines the co-opting of neutral or pastoral concepts such as "climate" and "ecology." Of course, the word "green"

no longer denotes a colour among other
colours within a neutral spectrum.

A CBC documentary made no attempt to
be impartial when a trembly-voiced narrator
recounted how the couple had to leave their
farm and move to Regina.

**The public broadcaster morphs "news"
into tropes representing a form of nostalgia
for quasi-knowledge free of error and illusion.**

4.

Over 15 million tonnes of carbon dioxide
have been pumped underground. No test
results support claims that CO^2 has migrated
through geological storage.

**Young wolves are acting on naïve
ideology proposed by icons like David Suzuki
who organized the wreckage of the "hippies"
into massive concentration camps.**

The project covers some 52,000 acres
with a total of 963 active wells; 171 injection
systems. Overall it is anticipated that some 20
Mt of CO^2 will be permanently sequestered.

**Suzuki et al created a generation
of idealists unable to distinguish carbon
sequestration from their own prison of
enviromancy. Lenin lived in such a zone
of exile in 1898, and Chekhov visited an
activist colony on the Sakhalin Islands.**

5.

Even the *Calgary Herald* joined the global
media inquisition at the Conn family
conference.

**We must understand how small
individuals, the microbodies of discipline
deploy unexamined tactics (school recycling
programs, litter clean-up projects).**

Environmental despotism has
reached the courts which fined Syncrude
more than 3 million for the unintentional
death of ducks on its tailings ponds.

**One can link "justice" and the
transformation of children's bodies into
highly complex systems of manipulation
and conditioning.**

6.

Organizations we considered allies
called for greater government oversight
without citing Industry's comprehensive
seven-page report.

**Only precise analysis can excise
the desire of the masses for activism and
reveal public complicity in the refusal to
decipher what environmentalism
(enviromancy) really means.**

As an industry we must wrest
the media from its addiction to activist
sensationalism and present our own
isotopes.

The good news is that now
a majority, possessing an economic
plan can dismantle the social and
cultural hegemony in which activism
operates in our own heads.

from *filling Station*

Palliative Care Reflective Portfolio

for PJ

i.

Do I? Admit to the neighbour I need help?
She'll offer impatience, weak Earl Grey.
So I get admitted, impatiently, instead
to an off-grey medicine ward with
Hospitalists who chart my chest rattle.
I suffer no fear for I am the recipient
of patient-centred, evidence-based, care.
This promise made to me, and me alone,
on a wipe-able poster reinforced by
a tenderly chosen stock photo, paired
with a font inspired by Cezanne's cursive.
I curse the machine hum, the urine pain,
the *C. diff* sour smell, the pump noise,
the infection control, latex-free signage.
Only last summer the lake removed such
anguish, or else it was the icy three gin
and tonics, the wind, your beautiful neck.

I presented to the ER with severe pain
in my lower, well—does it really matter
where this began? Things have evolved.
Let's keep up, I say. But he presses me.
Read the chart I bark. He does, and utters,
back, left flank. There. I am incapacitated.
Last summer I was myself, that recently,
really, independent, with plans in place.

I golfed. Was a snowbird. I hear this,
my evaporating life as chart notes.
The biography that no one considered
worth penning—bit late for sad thoughts.

You dear, are elsewhere, gone in that
peculiar way—off the wall, in a facility
with advanced dementia. At the lake
last summer your dress removed one
afternoon for no reason and we stared
at one another until we remembered
the way it was done, by us. That was the last
time our bodies knew their lines. First?
Another century. Same lake. We giggled—
poke, poke, poke. The results of
investigations indicate—no wait for it,
I require a biopsy of the ilium lesion
for a definitive diagnosis, but a working
one: metastatic renal cell carcinoma.
It's explained to me in grave tones,
with colourful grace notes—because
some do not know, I know, the meaning.

ii.

Before a doctor dies, he becomes a person.
Mortality being a pre-requisite for death,
this occurs to me. My goals: pain relief,
symptom control. Not curative. I do not
speak but agree by blinking to this plan.
My son has arrived. He is a doctor too.
He has a new wife. Younger, a prototype

of the previous, luxurious version.
Their language is useless here because
I still understand it, even if I can no longer—

The resident's mind is so fresh it's still setting.
What are the words for the thing I want to say?
I try whisper to him, and he leans in,
I try to whisper to him: *Give me an overdose.*
He looks aghast. Did I manage to speak?
He says, what I am about to share is going
to be difficult to hear. My son and the resident
are speaking. I am still, listening. The cancer.
Likely metastatic. Left kidney. Multiple locations.

My next steps are to determine I cannot walk.
My son's first steps—that rock ledge at the lake.
Radiation might be an option for symptom control.
It is not a cure. They discuss goals for my care.
My son takes the news hard. He is emotional.
He is relying on his child-wife for comfort,
condolence, I use my eyes to indicate Kleenex
without meaning, it has a tone of reprimand.
Comfort is assured. Remembering questions
can be hard. Try to write them down.
Pain and symptom teams get involved
and former colleagues in Radiation
Oncology and Orthopedics are called upon.
Or maybe they are just visitors. They see
themselves in me. Smile. The first week
the pain begins to modestly improve,
I am told.

      I walk a length of the hospital
ward with discomfort, I am told.

Options for care outside of the hospital
are discussed, I am told. I cannot return
home. I cannot not be cared for, at my son's
home—for a reason never explained.
I wish to be reunited with my wife,
but I cannot speak. A social worker
I once was rude to intuits what
no one else can and applies for spousal
reunification on compassionate grounds.
I apologize to her all night.

The resident finished his rotation today.
Dictated, in all seriousness, into his small
machine final thoughts for his Palliative Care
Reflective Portfolio: *The patient is optimistic
he might be discharged to his demented wife.*

from *The Puritan*

JEFF BLACKMAN ◆

The Prime Minister shook his son's hand

Memory need not necessitate
mention, you gosh-daughters
and gosh-sons of television.

from *The Steel Chisel*

Two Fish

Say you have two goldfish, pet-store
fishlets bought for 25-cents each, carried
home in a plastic bag and nurtured for years.
Let's say you clean the tank, place each fish
in its own half-filled Mason jar, each
a bit small for large fish, but adequate
for the short time it should take to balance
the tank's pH. Suppose you put the jars on a very
high shelf, then forget they're there for months,
until most of the water has evaporated, until
what's left of the fish-shapes surrenders
to the dictates of the jars, becoming two squat
cyphers of twisted life. Let's say that's how
you find them, your heart swelling with shame,
and quickly, with shaking hands, pour them
back into the tank. Which is more alarming?
The fish who sinks to the bottom, distorted
as in a funhouse mirror, one eye bulging
to the size of its chest, fins extruding
from the wrong places, who squats there
staring out, steady as a barrel? Or the one
who reconstitutes itself as a sponge takes
on tap water, who swims off briskly,
picking up and dropping bits of gravel
with its fish lips, foraging with little
clicks, as it always did before? Which?
The hideously damaged one, or the one
who moves on as if this was what it meant
to be entrusted to your care? Which fish?

from *Hazlitt*

CHAD CAMPBELL ❧

Concussed

An act of dislocation, those first stricken weeks.
Some I remember. The Irish man, Tom, pistoning
the thick muscle of his arms in the air after one
old friend or another mocked his recovery, his exile
from the bars, his little room in his mother's house.
Weeks are a wash of introductions: drugs of choice,
dates since the last use. This is a room of the earliest
recovery, days so young not even the traitorous
dreams have come for you yet, when the craving
mind concocts its own visions of using & you wake
in sheets of sweat, gums numb, teeth set. Deprived
of ecstasy, a crushed filament, the air there is sore,
the time of day aches as light shuddering in
the trees comes concussed & I don't remember
many of them there with me, a few stories, the sense
everywhere of families pressing, praying. & I'm sure
they don't remember me. Just another set of hands,
shifting feet, a twitch of involuntary muscle. &
when a newcomer breaks the rule of description
speaks the drug too plainly, too vividly, the phrases
shine like a flashlight at a tree line, a moment all your
eyes flare: wolf: there you are, we think, there you are.

from *The Puritan*

The *New York Times* Uncovers Arson

"Slaves packed that burning house.
It was—I tell you—the worst weekend.

"Under a flame-scorched moon,
so many howling, weeping souls had Hell right here,
and came to char and ash and smoke.
It was pitiful, pitiful.

"Not even our most anxious guitars
get close to the precise noise
an infant makes
as fire eats through the flesh,
turning the body
into a coffin—
no—just an urn for ash.

"The flaming, perishing 'niggers'
looked like they were renouncing flesh
to become perfume.

"Torrid immolation was their church.

"These 'runaways' had sheltered in the decrepit homestead
near Charleston,
but were betrayed,
and once betrayed, trapped,
and once trapped,
eligible to be destroyed.

"(The intact bodies looked like blackened fish—
fat, juicy, charred.)

"The night was ash, roars, crackles, crying,
moon, timbers, flames, embers, tar…

"Under the ragged moon,
Reality turned jagged;
Living beings got snagged:
A shimmering mishmash—
a night of flame and ash—
heart-strings sagged out-of-tune.

"The fire erected a barrier of light.

"Against the darkness, a pure pitch-colour,
the blazing house resembled a bird cage,
suspended, set afloat, close to earth,
as beams snapped, floors caved in,
and ex-slaves quit hollering
in their *de facto* prison,
and settled down to incineration.

"To be Romantic, when some jumped,
flaming from windows,
becoming chimeras of light,
you could say
they were foolish, carnal saints,
electing martyrdom over servitude.

"Or you could say they were bogus migrants,
fake refugees,
seditionists against The Republic,
and fraud artists in their claims of ill-treatment.

"(Many do skedaddle to *Gam Sham*[1]
in spidery caravans,
lurking, hiding, scurrying,
infiltrating nooks, crannies of woods,
as discreetly as poisons
slip into soups.)

"You could number them as 'subhuman devils.'

"Yet, my nightmare privilege was to hear—
mid hectic roaring—
each crackling diminuendo of the darkies.

"The moon was more bronze than ivory.
Then showered down indifferent starlight.

"Anyhow, when the sun come up,
only dust rose too,
and I saw a taciturn piece of roof—
Futility in all that quiet.

"Raking the embers, I felt sick to find
a prune-shaped man who'd burst open,
his guts frying like all the pork
he likely loved to eat.
I found also a body singed hairless—
resembling a black jujube candy
or a twist of licorice.

---

[1] Cantonese: Gold Mountain (i.e. Canada).

"One mother had a tarpaper spine;
her face was a charred shoe.

"I even stepped on—and squashed—a heart.
It had been burnt, but not the blood still within.
It squirted out as my foot pressed down
on the slippery, dirty flesh.

"I had to navigate fluid meat.

"The house had largely broken down.
The dead were largely invisible under my bootsteps.
They were scraps—silent scraps—of *Nothing*.

"Unexpected feces did crop up—
here and there—
a kind of dark, cherry mash.

"I stumbled over a hybrid body,
a mulatto weeping caramel:
His cadaver was a patchwork puzzle.

"I noticed a babe already a lantern
of lustrous flies,
incommensurably putrid.

"Then, the sun was iron;
the house was a shadowy clearing;
or a bitter orchard.

"The burnt-over area resembles gravestone shale
or a tar oasis.

"I did not infringe upon any house of light:
Only a carnal loss.

"I couldn't linger in the hot wreckage—
lest I put my clothes to flame.

"There was a dissipated breeze—
a lot of charred nudity—
and lacerating sunlight.

"How could my remorse
be any more passionate than Morse Code?

"In this South Carolina forest—
swamp, lilacs, and mosquitoes—
these people have made a pitiful finish.

"None of this report takes sides
in the disputation over *Slavery.*

"Yes, the environ was horrid,
the event, horrid.

"But we all die:
Green maple leaves turn gold maple leaves.

"Even doves go into the furnace—
the cold ash pit that is the grave.

"Sooner or later, our letters are smoke,
and our dark dreams
are illuminated by worms.

"No crows will fuss over this burnt meat."

[Tessera (Italy) 24 *septembre* MMXII]

from *Grain*

LUCAS CRAWFORD ❧

Failed Séances for Rita MacNeil (1944-2013)

We are all
the weary travelers
Traveling traveling on
　　—Rita MacNeil

I
Rita, you requested that your ashes
be held in a teapot—"two if necessary"
Low days, I browse plus-size caskets
(They are all pink or blue)
But you took death with milk and sugar, long steep
　　　　Rita, we are both members of the fat neo-Scottish diaspora.
　　　　Don't tell me it doesn't exist, sweet darlin'
　　　　until you are the only fat transsexual
　　　　at a Rankin Family concert in Montreal.
　　　　Until you feel more at home than you have all year
　　　　when Raylene (1960-2012) thumbs-ups
　　　　your 400-pound dance moves in the front row
　　　　during that last, last, encore.
　　　　　　　Fare thee well, love.
　　　　　　　Will we never meet again no more?

II
In Grade Two, I sang with your coal mining choir, "The Men of the Deeps"
There is something terrifying about one-hundred pre-pubescent squirts
squeaking out the high falsetto tones of "We Rise Again"
over the miners' sea of too-knowing bass tones.

The highest note of the song comes at the word "child"
and we screamed it. We didn't yet have the sadness
that keeps you from even trying the high notes in that tune,
which take you from ours to other worlds and back again.

One of the miners comes forward in concerts for a mustachioed solo
I heard him on the CBC the day you died, having an open cry
They all wear helmets onstage. They are all Henny Penny
ever hardhat-ready for another falling sky.

Rita, did I ever tell you my great uncle Miley died in the mines?
My mother and I drove to Glace Bay last year
The old company houses are split down the middle
Each half is a different hand-painted hue and empty

We bowled candlepin alone in the basement of a church
It did not strike us to genuflect upon entry

III
Rita, I heard the RCMP trailed you in the '70s!
They were not good Arts reviewers, those Mounties:

*She's the one who composes and sings women's lib songs. 100 sweating,
uncombed women standing around in the middle of the floor with their arms
around each other crying sisterhood and dancing.*

They didn't know the *gravitas* required of a fat woman with a microphone.
They didn't see you as a teenager with a baby decades before *Juno*
Or the surgeries you had for cleft palate in your youth
Not even the abuse you sang through

They don't believe in ghosts like we do or know those family spirits
that can refill a rum tumbler when your back is turned.

IV
Rita, do you remember the "Heritage" commercial about mine collapse?
An actor swears that they sang   those   hymns
Even drank their own *you know*

At seven, this frightened me
But now I've seen a bit
I've watched Ashley MacIsaac (1975–) discuss urination during sex
I still toe-tap to his first crossover hit
Still watch the bit on Conan O'Brien
where Ashley kicks up his kilt
while going commando.
Yes, to queer kids watching at home
a kilt can become a portal to another life
not yet witnessed or understood.
Step we gaily, on we go!

Heel for heel and toe for toe!
I want to feel him move his bow, dab at his brow,
wash his feet, or at least buy him a pedicure
so that I can tell him that the queer, rural Nova Scotian diaspora
            (don't tell me it doesn't exist, b'y)
needs him to survive because
my accent is buried in Banff now
and he's the last member of my trinity still,
last I checked, alive.

V
One of my fat aunts resembles you, Rita.
Once, at the liquor store, someone cried:
I didn't know that you're in town for a show!
My aunt grabbed her rye and tried to smile
She drove home angry foot to floor
had her niece pour the spirit
until the ice would float.

Now she's on the wagon.
Her niece is a nephew.
Things change, Rita.

Rita, say anything! Tell me we can break biscuits
with blueberries and Devonshire cream.

Say that you'll let pitch-free me
hum along as you sing me to sleep.

Just don't tell me we didn't exist
Don't tell me you don't
feel the same way too

from *Room*

Ulysses

The book you were always planning
to finish, that beautiful boxed edition
mounted on a tripod, displayed on a shelf
across the room from your library wall,
the thousands of books you've already read,
thoughtful lines highlighted, certain poems
marked with ticks in the table of contents,
I could see that book tossed in the river,
the long winter's ice broken at last,
floes grating against one another, peeling
rushes and brush from the banks,
ice jammed at the turn, piled high,
water rising, rising, slabs of ice driven
over other slabs of ice, some thrust
above the banks, sliding across the road
or slamming trees, tearing them loose from shore.
Downstream the footbridge at the golf course
is battered, it convulses, collapses, is carried away.
Amidst the grinding ice, the sound like mourners
beginning to wail, your book rides the current,
its box like a boat to keep it afloat in the surge,
it bounces between giant wedges of ice, bobs
along on the torrent, eludes a falling tree,
sweeps past a floating bench, around a tangle
of brush on the curve and out of sight, shots
of the April flood filling the suppertime news
and not a word of your funeral.

from *CV2*

That Great Burgundy-Upholstered Beacon of Dependability

Over dinner, my landlady laughs about her day
teaching rich Korean kids the difference
between nightstand and one-night stand.
Her son goes wild for the bicycle pump.
From his high chair, he wails for it, erupting
borscht. Two years old and he refuses to sit
without its hard plastic denting his chin.
I don't get relationships. Once I got lace
panties in the mail from a friend who lives
in Winnipeg. He wrote, *I'm coming to visit
you at Christmas!* So I spent December
avoiding him, pretending to be busy, ice-skating
until my feet purpled, wondering how love
could transpire so oppositely between two
people. My mother once loved a grey van
so completely she sat in it for twenty minutes
every winter morning while it defrosted.
They listened to the radio together, to her
favourite tapes. The van went everywhere
with her, unlike my father who plays poker.
It lived for thirteen years in our driveway,
a great burgundy-upholstered beacon
of dependability, until its engine went.
I want to climb into you and strap myself
in, but that's not really love. Instead,
we idle in separate uncertainties, exhausting
reassurances. You thank my landlady
for dinner and roll away into a night
that imperfectly intersects my own, and I try

to stop imagining the ways we could fail
each other, and the people in rooms
everywhere who are continually failing
each other, and hope towards someday
having one nightstand with you, maybe two.

from *The Fiddlehead*

Mannequins

In the lingerie store, modest mannequins
      are left overnight without a stitch, plastic breasts pristine
          under security lighting.

Full-bodied bodies—the upper echelon—
      slouch in windows, their tapered fingers
          to their turpentine lips,

maternity models swell indefinitely,
      bellies full of unborn air.

Synthetic beach-goers and their simulated sand,
      outdoorsy types perched on compressed Everests,
          fashionable nouveau riche bored to complete stillness.

Female mannequins are given hair 43%
      more often than their male counterparts.
          And earn less money.

Their relations are bludgeoned in CPR classes,
      painted black and white and thrown through car windshields,
          ordered online

and, for a brief period in the '50s,
      became the mutilated aftermath of faux nuclear bombs.

Mannequin folklore is rich and staunchly guarded:
      the man with idle hands in Sears,

the Paris girls who made it into a magazine
        as part of an exposé on eating disorders,

where the retired torso pros go
        to buy heads and arms and ankles
                and take up bland professions:
                        pharmacy, accounting, law.

from *Poetry is Dead*

Lesbian at a Bachelor Party

There is a cigarette burn in this red velvet chaise. Where can I touch her? This red velvet chaise smells like feet. Where can't I touch her? She's so familiar. She's so beautiful it must be a burden. I've always considered the female body to be sacred. Smells like feet stink and mothballs. The men totally have boners. She has 100 fucking dollars between her legs. Bachelor parties mean pay up. Are my hips grinding involuntarily? Keep your hips still. Breathe through your nose. Arch your back. I guess I've always considered myself a failed female. What's wrong with my body? I wonder what Radclyffe and Una did in bed? Only touch her on the places she touches you. Hair. Cheeks. Lips. She's my age; I bet we went to school together. Amaretto. Irish Coffee. Tequila shooters. Do I have the word "lesbo" written on my forehead, or something? How much have I had to drink tonight? The word "pervert." There go her panties flying through the air. Men yip like backwoods coyotes. The word "sodomite." Her pussy is only a slit, an innie. Don't stare at it even if it's perfect. Shoulders. Neck. Breasts. June absolutely must have penetrated Anaïs—muses hit the g-spot, right? Muse mean wet mess. What time is it anyway? We were in the same grade together, the same homeroom. Before sunrise I bet I'll find her in the pages of my yearbook. My best friend is wearing her panties on his head. Those coyotes. Her thighs. Her thighs. Her thighs. What is wrong with my body?

"For another fifty bucks, I'll pretend we're alone in your bedroom," she says. The men have undone their pants. "We'll just close our eyes, won't we?"

from *Poetry is Dead*

East Side Gallery, Mühlenstrasse, Berlin

I would have popped a hernia if I'd done
what I wanted: wrapped my arms around the cold
slabs of stone and heaved. But a history of
failed superpowers made me feel weak.
I strolled the busy Berlin street, the longest
expanse of Wall still standing, freely
decorated with paintings and graffiti
from around the world: a Chilean hurrah,
a South African rainbow, an Australian
abstract part-fireworks, part-Einstein's hair.
The *thereness* of the site squeezed my breath into
something I could fit inside an envelope,
perhaps a secret cry for help. Yet carnivalesque
as well: explosions of colour, crowds snapping
photos of each other pressed up against the weight.
Back at the beginning, I slipped behind
the façade to the other side, the Death Strip,
where the wall wasn't festooned with triumph
and apology, just white slabs multiplied.
Less air held between your lips and lungs,
a square of folded tissue paper. Peering side
to side, then straight ahead, I tried to downgrade
the effect by using names like *lane* or *alley*
or even *tunnel* with its suggestion of escape.
But the Wall was one refusal
to compromise after another, as if
a mountain had been dismantled and laid
end to end throughout the entire city,
a force of stone hands held against both day
and night. I wanted to diminish my failed heave

into an exhausted embrace, place one cheek
against the cold until the whole side
of my face was numb. That alone
would have got me killed twenty years ago.
No comfort to be shared, the tourist wall
still casting shadows deep and lethal enough
to mistake for memory.

from *Descant*

Gift Horse

No old-time bonnets with eyelet trim;
this baby wasn't born yesteryear.
No plastic shoes. We eschew

things that scratch / bind / itch.
Ditto Velcro and rompers with
buttons up the back, sans front closures.

Please, nothing with cutesy
embroidered pseudo-French expressions
or amicable-looking snails

slithering amongst pastel-toned garden tools.
Nothing advertising an institution.
No fossil-fuel-eating-vehicle motifs.

Anything laden with thwarted dreams
(however bright, however lovely)
will be promptly set free to the Goodwill.

No mohair shrugs, pleather
skorts, animal prints,
rhinestones, fun-fur, pinstripes, no hint

of a life wasted or scripted.
Nothing too *girl*, nothing too *boy*.
Nothing redolent of upper crust.

Nothing sad, ugly, tired, prone to stain.
Nothing that reminds us of pain.

from *The New Quarterly*

White Noise Generator

for Amanda Todd

The autumn air feels guilt, the trees feel guilt, the cables
and the pixels, the birds and the ditch. A tornado forms,
tries to suck a ghost back down from its slow lift. Fails,
then roars through the town then the toward the next town
over. Makes a point to hit every billboard on the way.

Horses run through sea-foam, white horses running
through a calendar. The cold chemical smell of a
permanent marker squeaking over rectangles of
paper. A mood-ring on her hand rotating through the
spectrum. All the strength needed in the narration, the
thorn that digs deeper with the telling. What happened
and is happening and the strength needed still.

Friend request like a conch shell left on your doorstep.
Friend request like devil-horning every face in my old
yearbook while on the phone into the wee hours. Friend
request like would you like to see the portal I found in
the school's darkroom? Friend request like let's cover
ourselves in wet leaves and mud before math class.
Friend request like I'll be your white noise generator.

An ocean is a good listener. An ocean works the teen
suicide hotline 24-7 throughout the year. A conch shell
(stay with me) is a telephone.

Friend request like a poem typed in an empty chat-room
at the end of the night. Friend request like I got a rooftop,
a joint, and a handful of stars with your name on it.

Friend request like what is difficult is what is necessary
is what is actually listening to another human speaking.

Picture a pear tree in the middle of a wasteland where the
pear tree is you and the wasteland is the comment section.

Never interrupt a girl while she is trying to draw a
horse. Never laugh when she whisper-sings under her
breath walking across the soccer field. She may be
summoning dragons, she may be summoning them
against you.

Flashcards held in front of a window. Another then
another. Trust and we shall be the receiver; love and
we shall be the amplifier. Until the amplifier short
circuits, the windows blow out, and silence splashes
everywhere.

from *subTerrain*

Les Rues: Montreal

Berri

the balcony in July's sweet heat sucking
            your fingers we were high and fascinated
with difference of the other it seemed
hours with your fingers in my mouth seemed hours
up and down each one teeth against your knuckles

            waiting on the street's slim corner for me
you so immaculate in white and sun-
glasses neck rooted over your phone
a nun once glared me across this street my
            bright purple shorts inscribed too small on my
legs when I left you the whole city
was shaking *enragée* the nun so cool
in her baby-blue shift and wimple you
            and I have the same-sized hands remember

Resther

we didn't come here looking for a fight
            mais la bataille commence les lignes ils sont
écrivées entre les francophones et les
autres anglos students shaking with the weight
of their idealism enemies from Ford
            Nation *ou mes amis* living here for
half a cold decade turned away by the
interpreted code *le domicile*
c'est quoi ça le gouvernement change their
            gros collective mind if we don't move our tongues
to our mouths' roofs in the right *correcte* way

we had worn red boots and marched *les rues* in
thousands and they had loved us red paper
            squares clotted the sky like blossoms

Saint-Denis

all streets here more familiar after
        a bottle of *dépanneur* red yours
only two blocks out of my way it's not
enough to mind but enough to notice

walking down in the city's popular one
        a.m. light your old bedroom faces the
ambulance route of *Saint-Denis* shrieking and
unsleepable in summer all windows
open to the night in need trucks pouring
        into your third-story room the ugly
brown curtains you never did change that first
time all my limbs went numb and my face I
lost what control I entered with and went
        gargoyle on you under an empty turret

Saint-Dominique

you pulled me from a marching crowd you looked
        so crisp in your dress shirt ironed and tight
shorts beside the anarchists we didn't
touch till after dinner politeness
we decided to call it there is part

        of this old street you can't walk past without
recalling how we kissed you said for
hours in front of that fence *pas de vélos*
s.v.p. coming in the early light
        from Village bacchanals I never told

you I don't remember this let you
shake yourself alone on your way to
another part-time job imagining
        all the dark angles of my open mouth

Sherbrooke

we ran some walk-up stairs against the slam
of riot shields watched bar patrons shoved from
les terrasses a cloud of grey a crowd of men
a spurt of red one eye lost to the spray

we marched for that stitched-up hole we marched against
   Charest we haunted him in daylight I
marched for the sun that caught the hidden grey
in your black curls for memory of your
tired body slamming me against the wall

   your sweet heat my other rising ended
alone on an office carpet months
before the marches *so-so-so-*
solidarité how little we were
     willing to

  from *Numéro Cinq*

RICHARD GREENE ❧

You Must Remember This

In Memory of Kildare Dobbs, 1923-2013

*

I took your word for the durians: so sweet
inside though they stank. I will never eat
one now, I suppose, without you to prod me.
In the cold days when you were all at sea
you wandered among fruit and veg in markets
on Spadina, explained to me about kumquats,
opo squash, taro root, choy sum, lemongrass,
lotus root. You said Casanova would pass
his saddest days among thronged market stalls
in Venice, and draw strength from the vendors' calls
and their stacks of asparagus and artichokes.
You were comfortless, so you tended your jokes
like a garden—provision for the months of cold.
I first met you when you were suddenly old,
all your clocks reset to an eleventh hour.
A heart blockage required an easy cure
but your cardiologist almost killed you:
your leg turned black, and then weeks in ICU.
It sent you back to your poems, as in war years
when your verses sang in John Betjeman's ears.
A commando, you rhymed through convoy duty;
somewhere behind it was an Irish beauty,
the girl who died and for whom your life became
an elegy. You never told me her name.

*

The kids knew nothing of Bogey or Ingrid,
of having Paris or looking at you kid—
my young students who read your *Casablanca*.

Yet those girls from Karachi and Sri Lanka
and Beijing loved the poem, your sailor's story.
You told them you were for 'the glue factory'
in an email of greeting. It took a year,
for the end to come. But, then, I had never
known you except at the end which lasted long,
all our years of friendship. What you shared was song,
a strange minstrelsy in what you said or wrote.
For all your words, you gave yourself by note
or rhythm, like a jazz man who talks with his horn.
Was there just one song to say the heart is torn?
        Play it, Sam.

*

You were, I think, prisoner of memory—
always that sad business of the ivory:
Empire claimed you, sent you 'out' to Africa
to be a magistrate in Tanganyika,
but you did time over someone else's trophy,
a piece of tusk. Free, you placed the Atlantic
between yourself and your old father's frantic
nagging, and in Canada you made a name
by your books and voice, but always there was shame.
At our first lunch, you said, 'I think I'm a lost
vocation.' What way you missed and at what cost
I never asked. Grandson of a Dean, you knew
psalms and hymns and all common prayer, though belief
itself wore out. Now, fifteen years on, relief
is most of what you need, and at eighty-nine
you give your last few days to poems and morphine.
Still yourself, as one by one your organs fail,
you remember rings of bells and Coverdale:
Yea, the sparrow hath found her an house,
and the swallow a nest where she may lay her young.

Once again, I do not ask what I should make
of the sparrow and her house. Soon you don't wake.
Lungs still pulling, mouth circling round your last air,
you are fading. I kiss your forehead, Kildare.

from *Hazlitt*

Evil Brecken

Is what you reckon.
Upper lip, brindled. Pubes, lichen.
Brackish armpits; thigh-thickened

chicken. A wank on the way
to other women. Box on a stick;
wake of peckers. Stupid

with bravado yet brutally
forsaken by self. I rut
in her blood past the bracelets.

Fused sex to sex, pixel to pixel,
we sit together, shit together,
brandish our teats

like handkerchiefs, *oink oink*,
muddle in the bristly
bacon of us: wrecking-

ball vulva, this bathetic smile.
These brambly old hands.
Our sandpaper masturbation.

Booze keeps the wounds
clean and the brain
meaner. Brecken,

you're named after a dog.
Brecken, you cuckold
my time. Brecken, whose cock's

in our esophagus?
It sickens me
to take her in the mirror.

That's wrong—I'm not *taking* her.
She's choked me out. Bracken
to my lesser fern.

Or I'm the leather chew
she's breaking in.
Her nightly grinding

buckles the crackling
cheeks, pouches the jowls,
leaves black pudding

beneath the eyes.
Would you liken her
to her daddy? Something

a little manly? Or to the sag
of grandma's hip-sac reflection?
How I'm aching to dissect

the feckless veil of her—
shave her face off
my face, bride

to my suicide.
But I'm too bloody
vain to maim what's visible

above the neckline
and I can't be alone.
Goddammit, don't go.

Don't tell me my self-pity
is a bummer. Don't
leave. Don't say I'm both

the obstacle and the goal.
I'm my own heckler.
Brecken is what?

Freckled? Mulled wine?
Bluff? Slope rise,
hillside, dip, declivity,

depravity? To break?
To shake a feeling?
Mottled, hot, hoochy,

declining. How do you know
what's to your liking?
If you, unsuspecting,

met yourself, would you
recognize your Jekyll's hidden
side? Share a glass?

Dish on childhood neglect?
Finish each other's pretenses?
Hook up? Break up?

Bridle the fucker's brio?
Hack through varicose veins
that blacken the calf,

breaching cellulite? No—
I won't *pull myself together.*
I'm my own distraction.

There's a widening gulf
between each brazen
erection of I–I–I,

a whole brood of knockoffs
infecting me. These phantom
pregnancies I'm expecting.

Uterus, barbed. Tubes, *unheimlich.*
Pickled genes; paretic pelvis. *Brr,*
I need protecting…

Hush, my Brecken, lie down with me.
Lover, lecher, what beckons—your bestie,
penetrant, bloodline, heaven.

　　　from *Hazlitt*

The Tower

Lobkowicz Palace, Prague Castle

From the tower, Prague severs into little squares—orange
for roof, grey for sky, empty spaces for your fingers to wind
through. Windows wired off in case pigeons squat or people
jump. Below you the muddy river and more square stones,
the cemetery and its twelve heavy layers. Dead everywhere
and low clouds of rain. To get here, you climbed for hours
across Europe, dropped coins into hungry cathedral boxes,
stood with silent hands while other women crossed their hearts.
In the hostel dark they talk about first love and you sink into
yourself like a crowded grave. There's no room for your body here.
When you cry in Prague, everyone knows you're Jewish. Each grave
is a mask. You can stand at the top of the castle, look out over
the orange tiles and cry about your body, what you will return to,
the way she's been hurting you, how you know it has to stop.

from *Canadian Poetries*

Ballad of Blood Hotel

A film on Bill Callahan,
I was to be the soundwoman.
The director and I rode a limo through Manhattan
rented my equipment, then he queried what
I thought of every suit jacket he tried on at Kenneth Cole Reaction.

He insisted I sleep in
his one-bedroom apartment,
informed me we would share a room when we visited
Drag City. Why didn't I move to New York to become
his live-in assistant? He darkened when I said I had a concert ticket

and had plans that evening.
He filmed me, muttering
'I might not let you go, and who'd know if I didn't?'
I made a fake call to a 'friend' as proof
of someone who'd be waiting for me. There's footage of this.

Outside, from a sticky payphone,
I cold-called hotels getting *no, no, no*;
until a vacancy by the Hudson, a scoliotic mansion.
A man inside a bullet-proof terrarium, lined in wire,
with taped up chicken-scratch signs: No visitors in rooms.

TV show laugh tracks
ricocheted through the ingress.
Four locks. Inside, an open, double-hung window,
the faint waft of bleach. The sun-faded floor
highlighted a dark rectangle where the bed had long been.

A black cockroach
the size of a butterflied sausage
hustled across the plaster wall and clung
to the window screen. I pulled down the pane, trapped him
in the lower sash, and he body-drew a panicked infinity sign.

Sweat spurted
from my scalp as I staked
blattaria. Closet: One wire hanger.
Nightstand: Bible-less. Beneath the bed: Not one mote
of dust. Behind the headboard, instead of bugs, an inch-wide

ray of blood sprayed
down the wall, thick as a surveyor's
fluorescent cross on an arterial. A line
steadied by force, the splatter deviated from mean,
skewed left. An ax, no doubt, one blow, to a person prone.

I kneeled on the bed and wept
about Woody Allen, Joan Didion, even Billy Joel's
insipid hit, *A New York State of Mind.* A class action lawsuit
ought to be launched over decades of artists' propaganda that lures
you to New York, only to find yourself using a rooming house's

communal washroom,
where a man is asleep or expired
in a shower stall, door agape, water pelting his rump
like an Instagram of a foreign countryside. That's one way to escape.
Bill Callahan fired the filmmaker on the third day.

There's all this.
There's all this.
There's all this unedited tape.

from *Arc Poetry Magazine*

Disappointment

how many winter birds have arrived at the empty feeder
since you broke your arm, and what do you say

when your father asks, again, *who are these strangers*
watering your mother's lily-of-the-valley? uprooting

our centennial tree? is it only politeness that stops you
from reminding him that he is dead, that this moment

is a dream, and by the way it is certainly not summer?

an immigrant, he could never accept that life below zero

is ordinary, that any phenomenon, repeated fifty times,
becomes your life. do you think you are special? do you think

it is only your own husband, who, looking
over your shoulder as you write a poem, mistakes

its shape on the page for a grocery list and believes
you're planning to surprise him

with a birthday dinner?

    from *Matrix*

Io

Your mother will not know you, your father
will not know you, your sister and your brother
will not know you, you will be driven
far away and you will live
in exile; then one day you'll be
permitted to return. And they,
as if you'd never been transformed,
will welcome you with open arms,
will call you by your given name.
And that's when you'll feel the change.

from *The New Quarterly*

I Don't Bother Canning Peaches

There will be enough gas.

Trucks will come and they'll bring fruit.
There'll be enough produce mid-winter
for cities and cities of people.

The farmers of giant farms
use only the cleanest
pesticides that won't kill us
or make us ill.

The migrant workers won't revolt.
The sun will shine in California
and there will be enough rain.

Planes will keep crossing the clouds.
The news will report famine and war
in far off places but here in the snow
we'll eat limes and mangos.

Food will drop from the sky.

from *Poetry is Dead*

Some Men

A man wakes up
in a monastery
on a mountaintop
in Tibet,
having given all
his possessions away,
and cries out, "Dammit,
I'm still me!"
A man walks into
a martini bar
carrying a chainsaw
and we all wait
to see what will happen.
A priest, a rabbi,
and a Zen Buddhist
live in different neighbourhoods
and never meet.
A man says,
"Take my wife, please,
to the emergency room.
She is bleeding badly."
Several men
are running as fast
as they can
out of some
martini bar. Something
is happening inside.
A man wakes up
in America, filled
with joy at living
in this land of opportunity
where anyone, regardless
of class, race, or religion,
can grow up and

assassinate the President.
A man puts a cat
in a box, connects
the box to a tube
that contains a toxic
substance, connects
the tube's lid to
a mechanical arm
that is, in turn,
hooked up to a computer
that monitors an isotope
that may or may not
decay in the next
twelve seconds. The cat's name
is Simon. The whole time
the man is thinking to
himself that for
at least ten years
he has felt—not dead,
exactly, but
at the same time
not quite
entirely alive.

from *NewPoetry*

Lake Vostok From the Perspective of a Yeti Crab

The Russians are impatient.
They're serving seal meat
in the soviet canteen,
the coldest restaurant on earth.

But down here the oxygen is tender
We don't mind the sub glacial dark,
the atomic pressure;
We know no other season
or climate.

Still, some distraction would be nice.
Nothing lavish. A mysterious barnacle,
a visit from the pale octopus.
A small act of mercy
or even sex.

We're not ready for the age of air
of polar wind
and sunshine

We're self-sufficient
In our long blond arm hair
we've cultivated private hedges of bacteria
and communal lice.

Above the ice the drills have stopped.
Temperatures descend.
The Russians are homesick
which is a long word in their language.

They'll return in the spring to photograph
the hidden wells of Vostok
but for now the lake is still and rock blue
buried in darkness as permanent as winter.

from *The Puritan*

St. John's Burns Down for the Umpteenth Time

Let's say the fix was in. Let's say history,
being human and thus short on ideas,
made change from an old bag of tricks. Say this
was something reported as news
on a day when your life came to no good.
The new homeless drifting from row houses
along streets tamped down by the heedless
and paved in afterthought. Out of hollows
in the unkempt, out of Rabbittown and Rawlins Cross,
they weep like mountain runoff in spring
toward an intermittent stream, in numbers not seen
since an expiring dominion's last riot
when the representative nipped out the back and left masses
in siege of their own blank stares to empty their rage
on the architecture. Shopfronts and storm doors
remade in an image of asymmetry we repeatedly
inhabit. And though there's nowhere to really go, we have,
at least, been here before. We stop in convenience stores
for pull tabs, hole up in pubs on Water and George
that close their doors in accordance with bylaws
but keep serving to those lucky to be locked in.
We watch our favorite teams on big LCDs
as they succumb in sudden death, where we learn
to lose and be helpless about it. We sit,
feed the machines, stay one feral glance
from turning on ourselves. The draught taps, the underpasses
through scaffolding, the acceptance of a certain
steep downgrade in terrain all lead the way
to a zero hour we never set, but have somehow kept
and from which we'll start again. A city comes to light,
will reassemble behind us, finally up to code and arrayed
with hand-painted mailboxes and an impoverished selection
of heritage colours in hues of a terrifying nostalgia,
as we push into the projects of the West End,

the spaces that await us, to speak the words as scripted.
It makes little difference. The television bristles
in its web of static, and sunlight warms your unmade bed
as if someone you loved deeply just left it.
The way forward is more solitary but clearly defined,
and our consent in its direction can't be otherwise.

from *The Walrus*

Left

My old dog hauls herself awake to follow
          up and down stairs when I get chocolate,
a ripe plum, stays close as I read
          a letter about Michael, boy I met at camp
when I was fifteen. He was sick as a dog
          that summer, hospitals, colostomy. But he calmed
us all with his heart-to-hearts. Mine I hid,
          mostly from myself. When we kissed
I thought, here's a place to be admitted. For a time,
          when I pressed against railings, I believed
I was separate from what lay beyond. The body
          is an alibi when the mind roams. Years later,
he waited hours in a blizzard for my plane
          when I visited. We both had children then.

          I don't know what followed him
up and down his own stairs,
          what his days were like before he died, paralyzed
in a hospice, his mind clear, his children young.
          The ripe plum of his kiss, echo of his laugh
like my dog running close
          then bounding away. This can't be
all that's left: a face that smiles and leans towards me
          and lingers, but has nothing more to say.

from *The Impressment Gang*

Safely Home Pacific Western

Plot points that lit some childhoods like pier mount lighting:
the rogue, hirsute, endlessly American cop on a tryst
holding morality discharged in one hand;
that and everything I thought I was done with,
credits rolled, kaput, but nothing is done with.

I think: William Herschel, who sent his eye up like a cannonball
into the Pleiades, which was once called the Nebra,
and it banged around there until Uranus, gas giant,
which was first just called George, stepped out
and tipped its cowboy hat of meteors and dust.

Well, there are some things you just can't run away from.
Where are we in the long line of demotions?
Ptolemy's stars, sugar spatter on paper,
first loves who ferment in us, and the low, foaming
stout of no one's thought swilling, unswimmable, deep in the head…

So I close my eyes and board my own tour bus;
there's traffic there too and sometimes congestion.
With its track lighting and fully reclinable seats,
I sit back on my Safely Home Pacific Western
as its Crown corporation takes share in my head,

and I don't know what lane I merge into but I do,
and I can go to the Pleiades and look up and see them,
swing back through the Milky Way of five years—
that was harbouring secret addictions to astrology;
that was nights in damp bars with bass that hurt;

slow dancing at weddings leading to more weddings;
learning it's possible to be thoroughly haunted
by the lone fact that hippopotamus milk is pink.
That was a think piece in *Scientific American*:
a particle inside your body is not, strictly speaking, inside.

And us, lost, in First Canadian Place, half Parthenon
half hospital wing, with no one in sight. Woodward and Evans,
somewhere unmarked, once tweaked a glass globe
and carbon filament to make an incandescent bulb.
But nitrogen escaped. Edison bought the rights.

That was clearing a toll booth where a barrier arm lifts
and escarpment is just a duvet you throw over someone
who's sleeping longer and later than they said,
and Pleiades of dust swirl, like people tumbling somewhere
you lose your head band, like astronauts, but not,

in an asteroid belt of the things not that we just lost
but never felt departing. How did all that become so distant
in me? Just know that I only meant to turn left,
signalled, and suddenly was above a whole continent
in a drive so far and high I almost caught sight of the earth.

     from *Hazlitt*

Small Fierce Fact

our heroine comes from a long line of barren women, sparky girls who
could and did but never reaped for they had not sown despite all

efforts, our heroine's mother comes from a line of farm girls who
knew how it worked, but after her wedding wakes to July blood,

then August, and then she is next year country: no yield, no workforce,
without swell or glow, there's no crying, normal is as abnormal does

when it does it every month for twelve years, no matter how she lies
down and shakes her bones with his, nothing coalesces, no cell cluster

latches onto her, yes then, she tries the other way, she finds a girl who
cannot look or a girl who sits up to look at her baby but the nurses

press her down and shush, and arriving in a rush of paper a baby's a small
fierce fact, a red-faced shock, a factory producing fluid at both ends

while the social worker intones always remember she's yours, never
forget she's not, a baby's a bundle of contradictions, the sudden eventual

mother figured the odds on you, that's who, baby, you graduate to
heroine here, all those female generations end up with you in your cap

catching pop flies after dinner in the long light, you burning your diary and
cutting class, baby, cutting your hair otter-short, it's you, cutting your teeth

on stories like this one, cutting the rebop, cutting through the bullshit
to hear the tale of the chosen baby, cut from red cloth. it's you.

from *The New Quarterly*

The jeweller's made uncountable examples

Settled in a corona of late night
bedroom more muddy
Madawaska effluvia
than bachelor
             pad, sit

for a portrait of the self
as sea cucumber.

To accrete its themes,
search skin tag online.

No don't. Search nuzzling sponge.

I get it.
        Sex is magical,

as in, it requires
misdirection.

So cue the bi

sected shot: on one hand, tender
exposure

—sweet as a drunk palm
finding yours on a night walk—

on the other, impervious bravado,
unsolicited catcall
from darkling air.

Look,
        you say *I don't want
to be recognized,*

but don't you?

Oh, dear stranger qua stranger,
I hear the frequency
on which you hum.

I've seen the world's one
dick pic.

       Until I cottoned on

I thought the pleasure
was merely the pleasure

of putting your fingers
through a whole cake.

                 Now,
inching
my phone up my chest

as if peeking at a pocket pair—
through the flush
          I hear

put down your guard,
your smarmy talk, whatever
good you try to do

I'm pointing at you,
and you, all of you

all of you, every one.

    from *This*

Steeltown Songs

I.

All down the conveyor, the limes
bumped ends with a banged-up
mango and my checkout nerves.
Off work, soon. And then another

BOGO week, my lip gloss layered
on like sealant, a week of soap and fat
onion sacks hefted high to haggle
their worth. Nothing else to watch

but gas blots in a grimy overhang
of light, where a caravan of cabs
wear lit-up caps and idle more
smoke at smokers' backs.

II.

Sometimes the Axe-doused
after-school stock boys tackle
shelves with the force of a tag team,
sweaty and boastful in their show-off skill.

Brings it all back, though whether
it's them or just piss-warm coolant
from the on/off A/C, I couldn't say.
It's like ghost pains in a gangrened limb:

to spar with them! to flex with pumped-up steroid
pecs and vault them to the vertigo of ceiling tiles!
(all sense slashed by *4061-lettuce*, *4041-plums*,
and an old recognition that dawns on me like drink).

III.

The new-bruised limes bump on past
checkout, and I stutter "cash-debit-credit",
then see. Spit-thin girl. A spastic 16,
nearer to bald and pitted by pockmarks,

who still watches worms ooooze fatly in rain,
still skips a hopscotch to the chimes
on poor porches. Prue. Same grin—toothy,
lean of love—still half-stirring some

Cops and Robbers cool, half-known through
the soft swells of a roughed-up decade.
She is gaunt as sparerib in the
disaffected drought of June. Older, now.

IV.

Back then, me and Prue were coyotes.
Spooked mean and scrapping into fights,
we spat like it was our sole tiff with the mud-
plugged stone. Played tag, too, with the boys

(in roles, always Bad Guys or Mounties)
imagined other selves we'd rather be
jailed in a quarter hour twice daily. Back
in that cramped neighbourhood of knives,

Four Square was the thing each weekday:
a mangy tennis ball matted by dog drool
and hit over chalked-in lines. And dirt above all,
ingrained in denim, dusting a tanned crust of skin.

V.

Thursday Night Smackdown. These were
pay-per-view poets, gods of powdered cheese
and TV take-downs, and I knew war was a need
of skin. Broken bodies got tried on daily

like shin pads, mouth guards, never quite fitting
no matter how much their shapes got stretched
to *make* them fit. There were lives beyond lives,
sands beyond my little slit of beach and beer glass.

Wanted to earn belts myself someday. Or box,
The Meanest Bantamweight east of Toronto,
my triceps emboldened by barbells, blood,
and a bluish cancer courtesy of Maritime Steel.

VI.

Sometimes we skipped our chalked-in court,
our tire swing's welts of spit-out gum. Mondays
the dawn mist of strangers' pot did it—too much
bitter in the smell of sweet. Or too much sweet.

On those days we followed the ripped-up main road
like alley cats, strays mewing loudly for bones.
Past the dark, bloated bellies of trash bags brimming
with meat scraps, past chipped paint and chokeweed,

we wandered where train tracks scarred the town.
I dug for rail spikes loosed by boxcars while Prue
eyed the dank front of the building behind: self-storage
doors like little garages rusted shut and let lie for years.

VII.

Mildew, damp earth, plywood for windows,
a thin fire escape of warped gray boards.
Gang tags advertised the safety of standing,
so we left the earth and its spray-on bruises behind

to climb until ears popped and we saw in panorama.
The whole town: musty churches, the Liquor Commission,
and blue banks where the river swam its current
to trees. No rail, so we helped each other higher,

rocked like planes redirecting in air *higher*,
past gutters and patched-up doors. Busted boards
swayed below us like seesaws. Facing left: our North End,
the used mattress shop with just a bare spring on display.

VIII.

We saw it all: home, on Clover and Worth,
where the prefabs were mostly built of Insulbrick
and gin. Crushed-up cans in the mealy oaks.
There, we were one stock, whiteblackredbroke.

When the dizzy bloodrush of too much height
got Prue and we started to crawl back groundward,
we both thought past town lines we couldn't see.
And what might grow there. Dragged legs to Kwik-Way

where found change paid for half the counter:
nickel each for neon straws and grape-shaped gobs
dipped in sour sugar. Squinted hard and puckered
as we sucked. Like steeling for punches. Or for a kiss.

from *The Puritan*

Listen, Junebug

The day you were born, the recession was a real thing,
was really happening, even though Moscow and Istanbul
were seeing significant real estate booms. A pair of bombings
killed 15 in Pakistan, and Spain tilted a little to the middle.

Attorney General Spitzer, a polarizing and crusading man,
was running a prostitution ring in the Midwest, while Israel began
its ceasefire talks and Fat Joe the rapper had admitted to tax fraud.
This was the day Barack Obama abandoned Hillary Clinton

and ran for leader of the democratic party—soon to be the first
black president in history—publicly announcing, I don't know
how somebody who is in second place offers the vice presidency
to the person who's in first place. And late in the day, the scientific

community announced that non-human primates conveyed
meaning through call combinations, or morphemes, which are
linguistically defined as the smallest meaningful units in language;
for instance, a prefix such as "pre-" or a word such as "I."

from *The Humber Literary Review*

mîscacakânis

Watrous, 2012

you are my yearling. I have brought you here
to give to you the prairie, a place to be human

and small and at mercy. In the evenings, you sleep
and I breathe a scatter of Michif into the soles

of your feet. You are mîscacakânis
my little coyote, running along the scattered flatland

with your arms above your head. Screaming, casting
your long shadow out on the narrow railway line.

We taught you to swim in Lake Manitou, the weightless
surf, then washed the salt from our skin

in the outdoor shower. In the morning
I braided sweetgrass in your hair and then you ran

barefoot and unafraid, shaking the dew
from yellow canola. You drift off in the afternoon

smelling of soil and sweat, sunlight and crop.
I have brought you here

to give to you the only thing
there is. May you be wild here,

a girl-pup, mine
from long ago.

from *Room*

A.F. MORITZ

Entrances

Compelled to seek my end
where the chasms… I almost said
the chasms of night, but no, the chasms of
minor darkness, night's traces or residue
in a small city life: squares, paved paths, low walls
with cubes on the one side called the inside,
alleys on the other side called the outside

and a memory—rumor or legend—
called the edge or sometimes boundary or margin:
a space of wires flying between tall towers
that walk toward other cities without moving in the form
of giant grasshopper-men, silver and fragile,
and under their struts and strings sing dunes of amber
and whitening green scrub, wind-brushed: the waste land
rolling away, the home of summer mantises
and meadowlarks…

                Compelled to seek
my end here. And I say this. Not man
alone builds. The worm builds too,
builds with him and what she builds is
the space in earth the shape of the absence
of her body when her body will fail. Compelled,
but I think her life was pleasure
and struggle a pleasure and her death a source,
a presence in the soil. Under me
the concrete we so praise, its hard cracks forced
by time and the peaceful restive worm,
narrow chasms into which I poke.

from *The Malahat Review*

My daughter imitates A. Y. Jackson's "Road to Baie St. Paul"

But that free servitude still can pierce our hearts.
Our life is changed; their coming our beginning.
　　　—Edwin Muir

The life locked in pastoral: ramshackle barns the colour of varnish,
burnt roofs, fences that raise arms from their sides until their arms
fall exhausted upon the earth. The fences are angels and the farmhouses
containers for men and women who know the fields with nothing
but the horse and the plough.　　　　　　O send me your angels
now, I will fix them with the bit and set them to work upon the scene:
to make angel-forms in the snow. The mountains slumping in the background
are for farmers and wives to set lives against, to wonder how many days
it would take to climb the slope, if they would turn back and see their homes
imprinted in the snow of the fields, if they would turn to salt by turning around,
the salt cracking down the mountainside, the salt a true snow.
Then the work starts again and the trees for colour stand in place as guards.

The beautiful polices the most solemn passions. The only man who can be seen
is in the cold, coming home or clearing a path with his horse ahead.
My daughter built this place with its limited range, let the structures collapse
and lean, the ache of unseen men and women held in their places and homes,
not a brushstroke that identifies the Canadian Shield, her ancestry, or the man in view.
Who could it be, and where is this, and why? I think I've lived there all my life,
with no little girl to see, feeling the angels condescend to the scene
as guardians of the spare. *Take heart*, I tell the man, and *Hurry.*
Find them, make sure they are inside.

from *The Fiddlehead*

A Thousand Times You Lose Your Treasure

She mistook the munitions for fireworks

She said goodbye to her lover

She threw the photographs in the pond

She dressed as an 'old woman'

She shaved my head (my hair too light from the white father)

She took off her jewellery

She took in neighbours   but not by choice

She could have been labelled 'a counterrevolutionary'
            and dumped into a mass grave

She would have said that I wasn't her baby

Tet 1968

        from *Event*

Margaret Rose

The females of my family extolled
the virtues of our Queen, her cautious charm,
the opera glove that sheathed the guiding arm.
For this was ours, the Englishwoman's mould.

But Margaret, the microscopic waisted,
a mantrap by the age of seventeen,
slid underneath us like a submarine,
desired, gasped at, but at last outlasted.

Her sister's pleasing properness peered out
from mugs and jugs and stamps. She had the crown.
She never stooped to let the Empire down.
She never left the other sex in doubt.

But Margaret, the ruined and rapacious,
picked amongst the cricketers and rakes,
topless, fogged, a fountain of mistakes,
making cat food of the Windsor wishes.

The E2 tank slides further into battle,
waving stiffly from the Bentley's back,
warning certain women not to crack,
waiting for the rabble dust to settle

while Margaret, the taut and disappointed,
has sunk like squandered change into the shoals,
but in the murk, her eyes glow, purple coals.
To us, the normal, she is God's anointed.

from *The Walrus*

MICHAEL PACEY ❧

Lightbulb

Icon of pure idea. Screwed into a sphere of permanence
skin-thin, fragile as eggshell, yet suffused
with even light—a Platonic corona identical
to the thinking mind's delicate glow. Say,
above Henry's bulbous cartoon head, his second brain,
its single hair ablaze.

Naked, it suggests a folksy quality,
forever swinging its gaze
on unexpected corners of the past—corners lit
with the warm steady fire of your affection—
there was always one above your father
as you watched him work in basement or
garage (anywhere a bare bulb swings:
the genius of the place). A galvanic presence overseeing
these Rembrandt-amber scenes, his hands tarred
with grease, the small tools kept separate and clean.

At the store—selecting the shade—*Arctic Pearl*,
Creamed Cumulus, *Snow-Glare*, inscribed
in tiny script round their poll—the wattage, frosted or clear.
Then that delicious sensation walking out of the store,
as if you'd just bought bags of nothing,
cartons of air. Nestled inside
those egg-safe packets you coddle home:
the power to see your rooms with the light
of still life. Screw a few in just for fun,
put the rest in a bowl: a bowl of glass pears.
Jars of sun. Tiny amphitheatres filled to the brim
with a thousand matinees.

Installation's easy—the global sign for "a dim bulb"
—how many to construe those exaggerated threads?
Inside the candy-spun shell, tungsten filaments,

twin antennae yearn incandescent in a vacuum.
Your idea of home's within this soft white circuitry,
synapsing back and forth.

You catch its essence waking some morning
to find a light left on—see it up all night
worrying, keeping watch while you slept—
a conscience, consciousness. (You feel guilty.)
Giving the scene the third degree.
Like Picasso's *Guernica*—its single eye
witness to the nightmare below.

That moment when they expire:
you enter the room, flip the switch and Pop!
Apocalypse, wick thins, disintegrates,
the globe grows cold, grey as rink-ice,
a dark rot spreads up the stem. Shake it:
you hear broken bits of distant music—
sleigh-bells and pixie-dust, then
a little click.

from *The Fiddlehead*

After His Brother's Body Washed Ashore, Roman

After his brother's body washed ashore, Roman spent
time dog-sitting in the Outer Mission. There was the
pressing matter of his own body and what to do with it,
so he fed it intermittently, walked it like he walked the
dog, and washed its hands. The house was dominated
by a spiral staircase that he did not climb; in fact, he
eventually forgot the second floor existed. Outside, the
Town held a street fair. Women rubbed raw chickens with
paprika and locked them in barbecue cages; people in latex
handed out smoothie samples. Down the street elderly men
floated out of the nursing home like pressed flowers from
a novel, cotton balls scotch taped to the insides of their
arms. Inside the house, Roman made the plainest meals:
recipes consisting mostly of flour and water that he found
in a cookbook written by monks. He had this cookbook;
he had his mind's civilizing impulse, which is to say, his
resistance to self-indulgent grief; he had the radiance of his
memories, and the terrific rate at which they were fading.
At night the dog circled him warily but they were both
too afraid to lie down. One day a friend sent a Doctor,
and the Doctor ran her gold tipped fingers over Roman's
body, pressing lightly on his liver and lungs, lungs that
(he was ashamed to admit) had newly begun to feel like
they were filling with liquid. He despised his body for
engineering this sympathetic reaction. It was like that time
he had walked through the house and random objects (a
blender, a space heater, a garlic press) appeared to emit their
own light, like he was underwater, and pushing through
swaying weeds to find his brother. Roman thought this
delusion was grandiose and narcissistic. But as the Doctor
peered into his ears he allowed himself one memory. He
and his brother used to do something they called Famous
Dancing, though of course they were not famous and
it was not dancing: it was a kind of gymnastics routine
performed to *Swan Lake*. Being older and stronger, Roman

would lift and twirl his brother; they cartwheeled in unison, did back bends and splits. During the rare times they performed for their parents, to calm his nerves, Roman would retreat to the place that he and his brother were building together, every night before bed, in their shared mind. That uninhabited city they had designed, whispering back and forth between their bunk beds, with its defunct caramel factory and abandoned fairground and feral llama population: some llamas grave and funereal, some llamas with overbites. Roman always fell asleep first, during these nights of construction. Much as he tried to stay awake, he always faltered in his purpose, though he never wanted to leave his brother building their city, its race tracks and strip clubs and burger shacks, out loud, alone in the dark.

from *Lemon Hound*

SN1987AZT

A common year beginning in my memory.
By March, in dark pools beneath Lake Erie
And in the zinc mines of Kamioka Mining
& Smelting Company, Gifu Prefecture,
Neutrinos from a collapsing supergiant
On the outskirts of the Large Magellanic
Cloud, a nearby dwarf galaxy, caromed
Through sensitive, hyper-purified water.
I was eight years old. For the first time
In nearly four hundred years a supernova
Was visible to the naked eye from Las
Campanas Observatory, Chilean Andes,
To the Nōbi Plain, where the great sword-
Makers of the shogunates are remembered
And the clear river waters drawn for sake.
I was thirty-eight years old. That spring,
While night contracted to its most exquisite
Northern density, the decaying light grew
Brighter in its deep pool of space above
The Salish Sea and the Morton Salt girl
In her short smock and yellow Mary Janes
Who'd been walking that faded billboard
With her umbrella in the ever-sleet, outside
Fairport Harbour, Ohio, for so long she could no
Longer be seen by the commuters flowing
West along Route 2 to Cleveland.
I was sixty-eight years old. Then, in June,
After the persimmons bloomed in Gifu
And the Nagara River lipped its levies,
After doctors in Miami and New York City
First wrote scripts for low dose AZT,
A drug that inhibits reverse transcription
And production of complementary DNA,

That crystallizes into a salt superstructure,
As in the Morton mines below Lake Erie,
The light began to fade. I was ninety-eight.

from *The Walrus*

Dorm Room 214

Under the blown glass angels with gold-dipped heads,
strung up by their haloes, a poster of Rossetti's *Lilith*,
Klimt's *Kiss*, all magpied from "The Barn"—our
ashram swap shop, where almost anything you imagine
miraculously appears soon after you think of it. Like
the soda shoppe chair in front of the window where
the Pole likes to fuck me, at night, with the lights on.
And the sprawling threadbare chaise behind the gauzy
sarong wall, where one night, three of us completely
ignored Kubrick's *Eyes Wide Shut*, discovered what
yoga was really for—two Aussie girls and that French
cyclist with River Phoenix hair. This Dutch guy says
my place reminds him of a Turkish bazaar, a harem,
a Babylonian shrine. He likes to play harmonica in
the shower, admire his chest in that mosaiced mirror
above the sink, where the German wrote *ich liebe dich*
with my daughter's alphabet stickers, and I thought
German had a dirty ring to it. Half the ashram bed-
hops. So hard to say no. To say no seems… ungrateful.
Like refusing Godiva's chocolates, silk wedding saris,
a foot massage. The ashram *in*-words: yes and thank
you. Merci and oui, tak, ja, yeah, sure baby.

from *The Fiddlehead*

A Citizen Scientist's Life Cycle

In summer the culvert didn't seem so mean, just dried up like everything else.

1.
Pulsing darkness. A chorus without pause
issues forth from the culvert's mouth
as it does throughout the year, spring flows
peaking now, beating me and the metal both.
A bit dramatic perhaps, but that's me
these days, feeling my age, my crooked toes
digging at my boots like gophers fleeing
too late the strychnine found in their burrows.
The colourless and bitter can make life
one long convulsion, a violent rush
from end to end. I hear the half-
crack of my knee, wonder who in the bush
will note the trudge, the hunch, conduct yet
another survey. Just me, I bet.

2.
Another survey. Just me, I bet,
here in the ditch, listening for owls.
I set the timer for two minutes, forget
tick by tick as timed minds do when strict rules
demand stillness. Hearing the click of crowns
in the wind brings shivers. Black spruce are evil
queens in this light, or Baskerville's hounds
gnawing the wet hollow in which I dwell.
The alarm sounds. Then a long staccato
from the east, as if blood-crazed gundogs
are cheering the hounds on. God only knows
why an owl sounds like this, or why my legs
nearly buckle on impact, like a deer
gut-shot, heading for cover, the bluff near.

3.
Gut-shot, heading for cover, the bluff near:
life is a passage and here I am, prey
preying on fear. A hunter always fears
the animal inside that waits for the day
it reveals itself. A spring bear, hungry,
slow-hearted, ambles toward the bacon
grease and fish guts, chocolate cookies,
the spot I fail to scrub off my hands.
Standing here, I am bait. The smell lingers.
I am drawn to it as usual.
Down the road, I'm told, a trail cam captures
passing deer, the odd coyote, vultures, all
in black-and-white, like any memory.
I squatted there last week. Too much coffee.

4.
I squatted there last week. Too much coffee
shakes my grip, the camera, make images
blurry, the spruce grouse a brown streak. Sorry.
Believe me, the red combs above its eyes raged,
almost burned me, almost set the forest
alight. That's right, it was early morning,
I hadn't slept and the dew was less
heavy than the fog. There was no warning,
no calling, and I didn't see the root
over which I tripped, nor the crossing,
nor the culvert, though the sound trickled through
my ears. Weary, I heard something passing
close by, swore it was my soul taking leave
and there it was, a grouse in the leaves.

5.
And there it is. A grouse in the leaves
uncovers the unfashionable
Romantic, so rural and lost I wave
at my own reflection, pull the wool
tight around my neck and shiver at how
old the ripples make me look, how tired
I am, lame, trying to walk like Thoreau
and my Thoreauvian friends. A liar
must do much better than this, be much
more than a body given to pauses
to search through the field guide for a match.
The Latin name of this bird amazes
naturalists no end, so I'll act astonished
until I believe I'm astonished.

6.
Until I believe I'm astonished
I will stand here and suffer. I promised
myself I'd be more awake, attuned, pushed
aside branches, woods and ruins, but a mist
has settled in the low spots like mist does.
Spring is beautiful. I use beautiful
too much, more than allowed, just because
petulance contains a single petal,
and that's enough to bring forth the flower.
It blooms. A curse, this lack of subtlety.
Like the marsh marigold, it's pure
poison. That nectar summons flies and bees
and me! Things grow cruel in the perennial
surface runoff, the ephemeral pool.

7.
Surface runoff. The ephemeral pool.
Call it what you like. I'm up to my boot-
tops in snow melt, up to my ears in fools
who go on as if nothing else could suit
this April night. Perhaps the frogs are right
for here I stand in the cold among them,
too human to be any good, midnight
pressing certain stars into my brainstem.
It's calm now. The big dipper handles breath
gently, turns and washes it. True. The grave
forest covers up every little death
with another. I die a bit each day
behind this mask. The heart freezes and thaws,
pulsing darkness. A chorus without pause.

from *Canadian Poetries*

Thereafter

With a debt to the reporting of Christopher Ketcham and Rachel Aviv.

Thereafter the northern plains would be cattle country.
I had paid off my younger self speaking of the highly contaminated water.

The dust was slaloming through the postmodern footnotes.
The sandhill cranes etc had refused treatment.

A host country manipulated the climate to guarantee good vibes to visiting qualms.
Given that the leaked materials nearly trampling me continued to slow, I watched

the footage of passengers huddling on the wings of the floating aircraft, just so
I could be made serious by love and choreography.

There was a part of me that felt that if I got into a cab that said wicked,
it would take me to hell. Pretty much

the rest of that day a crane-claw opened and closed.
The horsemen chirped into the mouths of artificially whitening clouds.

The wind in this, that once felt too private, read from cue cards.
I was double-hearing the suicides, who never leave the stage, so as not to sleep.

Maybe Dante's goddamn mike was open—

from *Lemon Hound*

Escape from Statuary

It's no secret that some people wish they had a tail.
We're torn one by one from rolls of human Scotch tape
to be born. Why let anger dam your heart
and turn you into stone? Sunlight, rain is sorry.
Dark cloud, go study for the flood.

Congratulations! Your every whim brings light
to new dimensions. Even your farts are radiant blossoms
in the infrared dreamscape of the common vampire bat.

The human heart, despite its plumbing
and catalogue of attachments, can't signal before it turns
and must be followed closely if we wish to fly.
Helium, that frisky hothead and life of every party,
is running out. Why? Maybe you ask too many questions.
Maybe it's time to let the wind have your clothes.

from *Arc Poetry Magazine*

Nearly Blank Calendar

Her husband, needing a change,
   accepts the spoon
of pudding she nudges
   past his teeth.
Butterscotch. His surprised eyes.
   Some dribbles
from his chin onto his lap.
   The pants
are forty years old and shiny
   at the knee.

*

Step 2: Starting with
   the fingers
and working your way
   to the armpit,
wash and rinse one arm,
   dry it
with a warm towel, and
   cover it with
a blanket.

*

The face, its expressions
   are so changed,
it's easy to see he's not
   the man she—
but the hands, the wrists,
   the arms are
the same. The burned hair
   smell. Don't
talk about that. Leave that alone.

*

A nearly blank calendar
        on the nightstand.
No appointments in April.
        May 4: Throat
Test. May 5: Pay ConEd.
        May 6: Dr.
Dandi refer to OncGastro.
        May 15: Philharmonic,
in pencil, crossed out in pen.

*

Step 3: Remove bedclothes
        down to the patient's
waist. Wash and dry the chest
        and abdomen.
Cover the patient
        with a warm towel
or blanket as soon as his
        chest is clean.

*

Leave that out. What would
        you want
to tell a story like that for?
        Leave that out.
At Schroon Lake there
        was an Italian boy
I let kiss me under a pine
        tree. Sap
on my new blue blouse.

*

Tip. Nail. Pad. Print.
       Cuticle. Knuckle.
Distal Phalanx. Middle Phalanx.
      Proximal Phalanx.
Thumb. Index. Middle. Ring.
      Small. Life Line.
Love Line. Health Line. Palm.
      Thenar. Hypothenar.
Metacarpals. Carpals. Wrist.

*

This is the story you want
      to tell your
literary friends about me?
      It's not my
business but I think you
      could have made
a more interesting choice.
      Tell about
my father giving an Astor
      credit
at the Gristede's he managed.
      I kept the books
for him after school, and
      I know
she never paid up. Tell
      about how
I slept for years under
      a piano.

*

Boiled water. Rinsed skillet.
        Clean sheets.
Left over oatmeal. Aching legs.
        Pill case. Tissue.
Radio. Gave up hope. Breakfast.
        Two hours' sleep.
Stop it. Don't ask me more.
        When I'm dead
and you're sorting through the house,
        you can keep
the calendar, for all the good it'll do you.
        They give them
out at the bank for free.
        Thanks
for allowing us to serve you!

*

She would plant a heel
        on the base
of the sewing machine to lever
        him sideways
so she could sponge
        the bedsores
on his shoulders. How he
        would wince
and shiver. Don't say that.

*

I met a woman once who
          dated Hemingway.
Her name was Irene.
          They played tennis.
She had all these letters.
          You know
what she did with them? When
          the biographers
came calling, she *burned* them,
          that's what she did,
all but one.
          Which she framed.

from *The Fiddlehead*

For the Ski Jump at Canada Olympic Park, Calgary

You grew into your destiny
in the city's northwest, overlooking
a gas station, the KOA, a few acreages maybe
on the earliest suggestions of foothills,
we hardly remember what that was like.
It was before I was born into
what I think of as my life.

Development has flooded the scene,
Victory Christian Church Complex venting
emissions, a warehouse vaguely Bauhaus,
reservoir of modern open homeplans
risen nearly to your base.
Each time I return to the same place

it's different. The adjacent new
community of Crestmont tries to act natural
leaning on the hill, rife with claims, wearing
last year's colours in its awkward
final construction phase. In 1988
some people who've bought its houses
weren't yet alive. For them

you might as well be a product
of erosion. A natural event, without promise,
defined according to what is most durable
about you. Does it matter to us
if we're outlived by a minute
or a thousand years? I'm not saying it should.

You wandered away from insignia,
from the party of the symbolic imagination
and no one noticed. Hung with ads now,
the odd corporate zipline. Tourists

on the observation platform observe
the accelerating ritual of supply
and demand. A view makes us feel young.

Ideal conditions are a memory that pains
even a Finn. Competitors and their equipment
have evolved, the old ratios are untenable.
You've outlived your design.
Would need to be retrofitted for safety
and who has that kind of time.

from *Cordite Poetry Review* (Dual Issue with *Arc*)

ANNE MARIE TODKILL ❧

Strontium-90

Campaigning for peace, their mothers gathered teeth:
Too big for fairies now, but we can show the President
how wrong a thing is war, how poisonous
the test bombs blooming in deserts blowing closer.
What use, the baby/milk/deciduous teeth,
once shed as easily as leaves or tears,
unless to mail proof that death's particulates
have fallen on pastures, are rising like sap
in the tender limbs of children.
How sensibly the mothers of St. Louis
washed, dried, and sealed these tokens of belief
(whiff of blood, perhaps bacteria), and
thinking how quickly life's chances disappear
(but indulging, no doubt, in some relief: long done now,
the hot-cheeked days of teething, abruptly overdue
attempts at weaning) wrote intimate truths
on the survey cards (months on breast, on formula,
where born, where in utero), while their gap-gummed
warriors, still shocked by the tug when the worried root
released, tongued the small craters, noted the metal taste,
and pinned on their badges: *I gave my tooth to science.*

from *Arc Poetry Magazine*

To My Suicidal Husband

Please do not look for poetry
in your death. Your drowning or
hanging or tsunami of pills & booze
will not be poetic.

There is no residue of poetry
in a bloated cheek snagged by a fish hook,
in a cracked leather belt swaying
from a light fixture or in a sludge of vomit
protruding from your throat like a second tongue.

And certainly no poetry will fall
upon your devastated wife folding
the last pairs of your dirty underwear &
ignoring the phone on a Saturday night,
piles of pizza crusts on the coffee table,
one of your horror films running aimlessly
on the screen, wondering why you
never imagined her twitching hands,
the packing up of your extensive library,
or the signed book of your own poems,
To Priscila, my love, because nothing exists
without you, under her lumpy pillow, now
warm as soggy shoes left to dry in the sun, and
her sobbing the last of her suspect memories
of your tender eyes, your brisk, hunched
gait, the slow circling of your hands
across her belly, into the awful emptiness of
hangers, towels and toothbrush holders,
microwavable meals and refrigerator
reminders, because your imagination
failed to reconcile the oxymorons
of her & your death.

This is not poetry.
Trust me.
While I am still your wife, and not a warning.

There is nothing less poetic than your death.
And nothing more plain.

from *Cordite Poetry Review* (Dual Issue with *Arc*)

Kiviak, or, Delicacy in Greenland

Caught in long-necked nets, five hundred auks
are stuffed in a seal carcass and buried
under rocks until the nights have gone from jokes
to jabs to death threats and back again.

Flight stilled, eggs denied, the dead birds meditate
in their fatty sepulchre. That airless universe,
a slow cooker. Beaks and bones soften,
feathers melt.

Latitude and chance brought auks and seal
together, joined them in a process more intimate
than digestion. More like gestation.

The birds' bodies, crammed in their surrogate,
are undergoing a drowsy conversion,
gradual then sudden, from corpses
to incubators. The collective gasp
of sugars born again as ethanol.

Exhumed stone by stone, yanked through skin
in a sunlit C-section, the auks spread
their wings as scent. The fermented flesh,
full of vitamins and protein, is a promise
of long life to the bride and groom.

The hearts are slippery and taste like licorice.

from *Prairie Fire*

Depth

You come from the same direction that
they did: the misinformed,
the would-be heroes, unfirst
European sons who knew
how much a pickaxe weighed, the ones
who didn't. A hundred years later
and it's morning still, sun at your back: you're driving
down the highway, rich and female, in your unimaginable
car.

Two, three, a half a dozen
elevators at each siding once. Sometimes the same red
as the boxcars, more often white, and the one
your mother's generosity has helped preserve, the one
that's cresting the horizon, there, in the right-hand corner of your windscreen,
is a faded grayish-green. Alberta Wheat Pool, Pioneer,
Searle, UGG. Thousands of them
in the middle decades of the century. Last count
in Alberta, 169.
                    2000,
the year they started raising funds to save it,
they made a postcard, got a grant to pay a kid
to sit all summer at the office desk in case of tourists.
There were none.

A memory of its dimness (brilliant squares
of August sunshine that the wagon entered from
and drove back into): shafts
and levers creaking: an immense
Cartesian animal. Your mom says it was 1999
they closed all three. And then tore down
the other two. Weeds, and the windows
broken, even the little one five stories up.

The shock wave of that dream of ownership, that failure
of connection whose real name
we refuse
        still passing through,
        still passing through,
        violence descending
        with the northern twilight,
        Saturday night
        and nothing to do.

That craziness. Its disordering
of hope. It deranged us all,
three generations, sometimes four: the picket fence,
the pasture and its spotted cows, abstracted finally
to something more like cold hard cash.—For? Well,
maybe that vacation, we could get away, or get
an RV or an iPad. Get a wall-sized
LCD.

Weeds again now. Frost fence. The windows on the tower
boarded up. A small rock through the bottom left-hand
pane beside the office door, stopped by the sheet of plexiglass
inside. A hundred years, and it's still
August, sky the dusky blue that means
dry heat.
        Edward Hopper, what's to tell.
        Everything's just fine here,
        ordinary as hell.

Main Street. Vacant. Clean. The Dollar Store
closed up, the chiropractor and the flower shop. You drive
to Whitecourt now, or buy online. The Co-op and the Rexall
still in business, but the parking lot unused—
two half-tons and a single car perched at the curb.
Clean inside, too: linoleum a lustrous, dark and
unmarked forest green.

But she was right, my mom, to try to save
the elevator. Loyalty
isn't clinging, it's a way
to know. Long love, its fragile afterlife:
details that we can't forget.
What's coming
won't be human if it has
no ghost.

from *The Malahat Review*

JOHN WALL BARGER was born in New York City and grew up in Halifax. He has published three collections with Palimpsest Press, the second of which, *Hummingbird*, was a finalist for the Raymond Souster Award. His poems have appeared in *The Cincinnati Review, Rattle, Subtropics, The Malahat Review*, and The Montreal Prize *Global Poetry Anthology*.

Of "Urgent Message from the Captain of the Unicorn Hunters," Barger writes, "I came across the word 'auk' in *Ulysses* (Leopold Bloom is drowsing: 'Going to dark bed there was a square round Sinbad the Sailor roc's auk's egg in the night of the bed of all the auks of the rocs of Darkinbad the Brightdayler') and looked it up: an extinct bird. The great auk was a black and white flightless bird, a metre tall, with tiny wings, hunted for millennia for its feathers, pelt, meat, oil, and large eggs. The last one seen in Britain was on the islet of Stac an Armin, St Kilda, Scotland, in July 1844. Three local men tied it up and kept it alive for three days, till a storm appeared. Believing the great auk to be a witch causing the storm, they killed it with a stick. My poem arose out of a desire to have a conversation with those three men. It is also just about unicorns."

LESLEY BATTLER was born in Barrie, Ontario. Her work has been published in a wide range of journals, including *Arc, filling Station, Prism International, West Coast Line*. Her debut book of poetry, *Endangered Hydrocarbons*, came out in April 2015. She currently lives in Calgary and no longer works in the petrochemical industry.

Of "Truth, power and the politics of Carbon Capture," Battler writes, "While working in the oil and gas industry, I read a lot of trade magazines to keep up with new developments. Something that really struck me, though, was the tone of the editorials. They all followed the same aggrieved, resentful narrative; Big Oil persecuted by marauding activists and their media stooges. Then it occurred to me that this rhetoric is the normative language of the Harper government and the same 'us versus them' mindset informs their every move. 'Truth, power and the politics of Carbon Capture' just takes the next step, co-opting Foucault to legitimize this construct of a downtrodden oiligarchy."

JONATHAN BENNETT is the author of six books, including two collections of poetry, *Civil and Civic*, and *Here is my street, this tree I planted*. He is a winner of the K.M. Hunter Award. Born in Vancouver, raised in Sydney, Australia, Jonathan lives in the village of Keene, near Peterborough, Ontario.

Of "Palliative Care Reflective," Bennett writes, "What appeared in *The Puritan* is the first in a group of 'palliative' poems. It's in the voice of an old, dying physician. It's about the man's transition from doctor to patient, from subject matter expert to cancerous object. The raw material for this poem came to me in the form of a journal, written by an acquaintance—a young doctor. One day, he posted on Twitter that he'd just completed his palliative care rotation, but still had to complete his 'Palliative Care Reflective Portfolio.' I asked if I might be able to read it, and work with it. He agreed. The poem is wry in spots. This was there, in a way, in the original (in which the palliative patient was not a doctor at all). I also kept fragments of the original story, bent now to fit my new, invented characters... If writing is rewriting (this idea of overwriting and erasure, until the finished thing is its own structure and reason, and cannot be traced back to its first drafts or its initial, hesitant beginnings), then why not start with someone else's words as a first draft? That was my hope when a young doctor handed over his private work, thoughts, and feelings, and trusted me with them. By the end, it was wholly my own."

JEFF BLACKMAN grew up in Thornhill, Ontario, and has lived in Ottawa since 2003. He has authored and coauthored several chapbooks, including *Blizzard: Ottawa City Stories* (with Peter Gibbon, 2009), *So Long As The People Are People* (2013), and *Leg Brain* (with Justin Million, 2014). His poems have recently appeared in *Blacklock's Reporter*, *Bywords*, *In/Words*, and *The Steel Chisel*, as well as in *Five*, an anthology of new Ottawa poets from Apt. 9 Press (2014).

Of "The Prime Minister shook his son's hand," Blackman writes, "I apologize to anyone whom I prompted to search, 'Harper shakes son's hand,' and to have an opinion on said event. If you already knew, hasn't the pebble been such a bother all these years? Either way, by the time you read this another national election's been held. I hope we're okay."

JULIE BRUCK's most recent book is *Monkey Ranch* (Brick Books), which received the 2012 Governor General's Award for poetry. She lives in San Francisco.

Bruck writes, "'Two Fish' just flopped into my lap one day, like an ugly bottomfeeder. At first, I didn't know what to make of it, but when I read it at a Christian college in Ontario and half-jokingly challenged the audience to tell me what it was about, somebody said it was 'obviously about God.' That made me take another, less flippant (no pun intended) look at the poem. For the record, we did have two fish, and the younger fish died recently, but not from neglect. She was eleven years old, and was very well-loved. Now we have one fish."

CHAD CAMPBELL is a native Torontonian who teaches at the University of Iowa. His first collection, *Laws & Locks*, was published by Signal Editions in April of this year. A finalist for the 2013 Malahat Long Poem Prize, his poems have appeared in *Arc*, *The Puritan*, *Maisonneuve*, *The Walrus*, and *Brick*, among other magazines.

Campbell writes, "'Concussed' was a sort of entranceway to the subject of addiction, and to a place, the Centre for Addiction and Mental Health (CAMH) in Toronto, which I'd struggled to write about. In terms of *Laws & Locks*, which in part traces the lineage of mental illness in my family over 200 years, it was important to place myself within that history. A distant relative of mine, Christina, was sent to the same institution when it first opened as the Provincial Lunatic Asylum. There are a lot of confused and volatile feelings in early recovery, but in my experience that volatility is often portrayed in film or television hyperbolically—where people yell or throw chairs or something. It tends to be quieter than that, more interior, and sometimes, as people simply relayed their experiences or the events of the day, I would find myself forgetting what it was that brought us together. That relative calm can change when the standing rule about not describing the drug too vividly is broken—then you can often see, if briefly, the craving in each other's faces. That's what I was after with the end of the poem, a glimpse of the wolf."

GEORGE ELLIOTT CLARKE, O.C., O.N.S., Ph.D., the Poet Laureate of Toronto (2012-15), is an Africadian (African-Nova Scotian). A prize-winning poet, his 13th work is *Traverse* (Exile, 2014), an autobiographical poem. His forthcoming title is the epic poem, "Canticles," whose subject is slavery, etc., to be published in three separate books, over five years, beginning in Fall 2016. God willing…

Clarke writes, "'*The New York Times* Uncovers Arson' belongs to my epic-poem-in-progress, 'Canticles.' If all goes well, the third and final part of this poem-of-poems (my emphasis on the plural, *not* on any, truly impossible triumphalism) should appear in 2021, when I should be sixty-one and closer to the grave than my mother's womb. My epic's pivotal concern is slavery, which we rightly condemn, except that it was the economic engine that drove American and Western European wealth-accumulation for centuries. But my associate subject is the image of the 'black' in the Occident, from the historical Hannibal to the character Othello. Each 'Canticle' is written according to three Oulipo-like 'constraints': 1) none can be written in Toronto (my current home city); 2) all must be written in actual, fountain-pen ink; 3) usually—but not always—I shouldn't know my narrative or subject until after I have begun to write. The result, as in 'The New York Times Uncovers Arson,' is a tad magical, in that the poem began practically to write itself as I sat at a desk in a hotel room approximately five minutes by car from Marco Polo Airport, Venice, Italy. I have no idea whether the locale impinges on each 'Canticle' that I write. However, each one is—I guess—related to travel writing, or, rather, writing while travelling."

LUCAS CRAWFORD is from rural Nova Scotia and currently lives in Vancouver. Lucas is the author of Sideshow Concessions (Invisible Publishing, 2015), which won the 2015 Robert Kroetsch Award for Innovative Poetry. Lucas is also the author of The High Line Park Scavenger Hunt (Transgress Press, forthcoming), and an academic book, Transgender Architectonics (Ashgate, 2015). Lucas teaches gender studies and literature and is the 2015 Critic-in-Residence for CWILA (Canadian Women in the Literary Arts).

Of "Failed Séances for Rita MacNeil (1944-2013)," Crawford writes, "I drafted this poem in 2012 as part of a pair. Rita MacNeil owned a tearoom in Nova Scotia. 'Tearoom' was also a word used in some urban queer communities to denote public spaces where sex happens. As a queer small-town Nova Scotian, I am attached to both definitions of 'tearoom' and wanted to show that they might not be so unrelated. If public sex is about deciding that you ought to feel entitled to do unsanctioned things in the public sphere, well, there is scarcely anything less acceptable than being an unrepentant fat woman with a complex history who dares to take the stage and put her body on display. A year later, Rita died, and my upset led me to rewrite the poem. It was immediately clear that the Rita poem needed to 'fly on [its] own,' to quote one of her songs. I was a young fat girl for whom 'Rita MacNeil fat jokes' were not an uncommon presence. Now, as a genderqueer person living far from home, I felt a number of losses reverberate through Rita's death. I could not speak to her, but I wanted there to be a public record of her fatness being experienced as something that strengthened someone else, and in an unpredictable way. These are séances written by a person who doesn't quite believe in spirits, so the extent to which they 'fail' is uncertain. Instead of reaching Rita, I'm speaking to readers. Can a reader of poetry manifest a lost icon?"

ROBERT CURRIE lives in Moose Jaw, where he taught high school English for thirty years and from where he spent four exciting years travelling Saskatchewan as the province's third poet laureate. His first book of poems, *Diving into Fire*, was shortlisted for the now defunct Commonwealth Poetry Prize. His seventh, *The Days Run Away*, was published by Coteau Books in spring 2015.

Of "*Ulysses*," Currie writes, "Jane Kenyon once said, 'It's odd but true that there really is consolation from sad poems, and it's hard to know how that happens.' The poem, '*Ulysses*,' is the final one in a series I wrote about my good friend, Gary Hyland, and his horrendous struggle with ALS (Lou Gehrig's Disease), the poems being my way of dealing with, first, grief, and then, sadness. Gary was a wonderful teacher, a terrific poet and a well-known arts activist. In fact, he founded the Saskatchewan Festival of Words, helped found Coteau Books and the Sage Hill Writing Experience, and, because of his writing and volunteer activities, was named to the Order of Canada. According to legend, upheavals in nature often mark the deaths of great men. In Gary's case, nature was slow to react, but the Moose Jaw River did flood on the day of his funeral in April of 2011. The poem is my tribute to someone who was important and deserves to be remembered."

KAYLA CZAGA grew up in Kitimat and now lives in Vancouver, where she earned her MFA in Creative Writing at UBC. Her poetry, non-fiction and fiction have been published in *The Walrus, Best Canadian Poetry 2013, Room Magazine, Event* and *The Antigonish Review*, among others. Her first collection, *For Your Safety Please Hold On* (Nightwood Editions, 2014), was nominated for the Dorothy Livesay Poetry Prize and the Gerald Lampert Award.

Of "That Great Burgundy-Upholstered Beacon of Dependability," Czaga writes, "I love where language goes wrong. How quickly a household item becomes an innuendo. I feel like these near misses are where poetry occurs most frequently for me: snags in the usual snooze-fest of language that shimmer in their wrongness. That's where the poem began, one night with my housemate Mona, an ESL teacher, telling me about teaching one nightstand vs one-night stand. The rest of the poem tries to untangle that snag, the subtle difference between human and object. Mona's son loved a bicycle pump with an obsessive ferocity. My mom loved a van because her marriage was unsatisfying. It's easy to love an object which stays where you put it, unless a guardian is trying to yank it away and tuck you in, unless it dies in your driveway. It's hard to love a person who is walking away from you, who could die or cheat on you at any moment. It's really, really hard to aspire to love an object with another person."

EMILY DAVIDSON writes and works in Vancouver, far from her hometown of Saint John, NB. Her poems have appeared in *Arc, Descant, carte blanche, The Fiddlehead, Poetry is Dead, Room Magazine*, and *subTerrain*, and her fiction has been published in *Grain* and shortlisted for *The Malahat Review*'s 2013 Far Horizons Award for Short Fiction. She holds an MFA in Creative Writing from the University of British Columbia, and reviews for *Arc* and *Room Magazine*.

Davidson writes, "The spark for 'Mannequins' was a brief glimpse of a lingerie shop through a bus window. The mannequins on display—just torsos, in this case—had been left unadorned for the night, and something about the glow of plastic bodies on a quiet street was captivating and incongruous. Someone hadn't dressed them, and I found myself wondering—did they mind? And if they did—what could they do about it? And so they became people. With relatives and day jobs and aspirations. Their world expanded to include crash test dummies and Rescue Annes, gender politics and gossip. Where does a mannequin go after retirement? What kind of stories do they tell? Perhaps these moulded bodies that look just like us … *are* just like us. In many respects, this is a humorous poem about synthetic folk in shop windows. Light fare. Yet 'Mannequins' is actually a difficult poem to read aloud—there are handfuls of multisyllabic words, and lines like 'where the retired torso pros go' that are just begging for your mouth to make a mistake. The poem asks you to slow down, take a second look. It becomes an exercise in empathy, a moment to revisit the familiar and see its hidden potential. There is some sleight of hand in this piece in making what is usually an object into a subject. Mannequins are often designed to be anonymous, their features obscured so we can better imagine what we might look like in, say, those designer jeans, or that impressive kayak. But the mirror the mannequins hold up in this piece doesn't help us consume—it helps us contemplate."

AMBER DAWN is a writer living on unceded Indigenous land belonging to the Coast Salish peoples (incorporated Vancouver, Canada). Her book *How Poetry Saved My Life: A Hustler's Memoir* won the 2013 Vancouver Book Award. She is the author of the Lambda Award-winning novel *Sub Rosa*, and editor of the anthologies *Fist of the Spider Women: Tales of Fear and Queer Desire* and *With A Rough Tongue*. amberdawnwrites.com

Of "Lesbian at a Bachelor Party," Dawn writes, "I've hit the age where I am nostalgic for my hometown. Going back to the small community of Crystal Beach, Ontario in the present day is somehow not as romantic as I remember it. Besides the fact that I am now a forty-year old grump, the change is mainly due to the closure of the Crystal Beach Amusement Park in 1989, after which the community never quite recovered. One of the remaining tourist attractions in the surrounding areas is adult entertainment. I'm honoured that exotic dancers have kept my home stretch along the Niagara River vibrant. I wanted to create a renewed sense of local drama and memory through a series of monologue-like poems that feature dancers as romantic heroes. I wanted to show the flawed and tender encounters that may occur at strip clubs. I wanted to show that commerce and intimacy are both at odds and undeniably intertwined. 'Lesbian at a Bachelor Party' is the first of more to come."

BARRY DEMPSTER, twice nominated for the Governor General's Award, is the author of fourteen poetry collections. His book *The Burning Alphabet* won the Canadian Authors' Association Chalmers Award for Poetry in 2005. In 2010, he was a finalist for the Ontario Premier's Award for Excellence in the Arts and in 2014 he was nominated for the Trillium Award for his novel, *The Outside World*. His new poetry collection, *Disturbing the Buddha*, will be published in the spring of 2016.

Of "East Side Gallery, Mühlenstrasse, Berlin," Dempster writes, "There is no way to prepare for history to suddenly appear around a corner. We had taken the U-Bahn from our apartment on Friedrichstrasse overlooking the Spree with its boatloads of tourists. It was a fair hike from the subway station to the longest portion of the Berlin Wall still standing, enough distance for my expectations to rise and fall until I wasn't really sure what to anticipate. When the East Side Gallery finally appeared, it was, at first, a bit underwhelming. Other tourists did what tourists do so well: lend an almost celebratory atmosphere to everything from the Tower of London to Anne Frank's attic in Amsterdam. The Mühlenstrasse remnants of the infamous Wall had the requisite postcard carousels and people posing for smiling photographs, but its relative smallness compared to what I'd seen on the news when the Wall actually came down back in 1989 made me bolder than I might have been otherwise. I strayed behind the first section, behind all the vibrant artwork, as anyone could have done and found myself all alone with history for several minutes, just the white stone devoid of any hopeful messages, the blindness that it was meant to simulate, the message that the space beyond was no longer available, that, in fact, it was where, for many, the world had ended."

SUSAN ELMSLIE was born in Brampton, Ontario, and has lived in Montreal for the last twenty years. Her first trade collection, *I, Nadja, and Other Poems* (Brick, 2006) won the A.M. Klein Poetry Prize and was shortlisted for the McAuslan First Book Prize, the Pat Lowther Memorial Award and a ReLit Award. Her poems have appeared in several Canadian journals, anthologies, and in a prize-winning chapbook, *When Your Body Takes to Trembling*. susanelmslie.org

Of "Gift Horse," Elmslie writes, "Before my baby's birth, I had a moment of anxiety, staring at rows of diapers in a store. I recalled 1980s diaper ads featuring 'blue pinstripes for boys and pink flowers for girls,' which suggested the company's lack of awareness of how these stereotypes would shape children's experience. Yet the gendering of colour is arbitrary: blue and pink designations for boys and girls were reversed up until the 1940s. Some things designed for babies seem so laden, not to mention impractical. The display in a university store of a pink onesie emblazoned with the words 'I hate my thighs' beside a caped blue onesie marked 'I'm Super!' made the news recently, suggesting not much has changed since the 1980s. My generous sisters gifted us with so many baby clothes that sorting and storing them took considerable energy. I felt uneasy about clothes inscribed with so much personality: tiny jeans with fur cuffs, university T-shirts. Would dressing an infant in these things shape who she'd become? Was I 'Making Plans for Nigel,' instead of being open to the person-in-process? Having another baby with special needs made me doubly aware of how a family's or community's dreams for a child are often inscribed in the clothes they bestow on him. Everyone hopes the best for a newborn, and any gift to welcome a baby celebrates a new life. I knew that, in resisting a gift's implications, I was 'looking a gift horse in the mouth,' but I couldn't stop looking."

RAOUL FERNANDES lives and writes in Vancouver. He completed the Writer's Studio at Simon Fraser University in 2009, was a finalist for the 2010 Bronwen Wallace Award, and a runner up in *subTerrain*'s Lush Triumphant Awards in 2013. He has been published in numerous literary journals and is an editor for the online poetry magazine *The Maynard*. His first collection of poems is *Transmitter and Receiver* (Nightwood Editions, 2015).

Of "White Noise Generator," Fernandes writes, "I started writing these fragments soon after watching Amanda Todd's devastating flash-card video of her story of being intensely harassed and manipulated online and off-line before she took her life in 2012. I felt the tragedy was the result of a succession of failures of empathy, especially the ones that happen in our current online realities, and especially towards women. Failures that we all make at varying degrees in all our lives. That's where I began. I rarely write about a very raw emotional event; usually I need to sit with it for a long time before I can do anything. So there's a kind of desperation in the parts of the poem. Oddly, perhaps, the first line that let me enter the poem was 'Never interrupt a girl when she is trying to draw a horse.' Her video was a powerful, heartbreaking piece of its own and matters more than my fractured attempt to come to terms with it. I think we have gained something immense from her strength and courage to share her story from the depths of that dark place. We cannot give back to her, but we can listen as hard as we can."

LISE GASTON grew up on the east and west coasts of Canada, and now lives in Berkeley, California. Her poems, essays, and reviews have appeared in a number of literary journals, including *Arc Poetry Magazine*, *The Fiddlehead*, *Lemon Hound*, *The Malahat Review*, *Numéro Cinq*, and *Prairie Fire*.

Of "Les Rues: Montreal," Gaston writes, "I spent three years in Montreal, as one of the many young transplants from elsewhere in Canada who descend on the art, bars, and schools of this coolest of cities. My time there coincided with the 2012 Quebec student protests over tuition increases and the cultural value of education, though this poem was drafted after I had moved away, and had returned, during a turbulent election season, on a nostalgic visit to the city. I wanted to explore some of the tensions between the individual and the collective, tensions comprised of cultural, linguistic or other differences. I was interested in how social exhilaration and revolutionary motivation can be simultaneously buoyed and undermined by individual desire. Like poetry, all of these attitudes must in turn negotiate with the threat, or promise, of failure. Formally, I wanted to play with these ideas through the loose, unrhymed sonnet, which carries its own tradition of lyric self-consciousness into this urban public space."

RICHARD GREENE is the author of four books of poetry. His collection *Boxing the Compass* won the Governor General's Literary Award for Poetry in 2010. His most recent volume, *Dante's House*, was published in 2013. Greene is the author of an internationally acclaimed biography of Edith Sitwell, and is now writing an authorized biography of Graham Greene. He is a professor of English and director of the MA in the Field of Creative Writing at the University of Toronto.

Greene writes, "'You Must Remember This' is an elegy for the Irish-Canadian writer Kildare Dobbs (1923-2013), who was my close friend for fifteen years. As a young man, Kildare was a promising poet, but after the war was briefly imprisoned for possession of ivory, a charge he rejected to the end of his life. He settled in Canada in 1952, becoming close friends with Mordecai Richler and Brian Moore, who regarded him as their equal. In his middle years he specialized in essays, travel writing, and fiction. He won a GG in the fiction category and six National Magazine Awards and was eventually inducted into the Order of Canada. As an old man, he returned to poetry, producing three substantial collections, *The Eleventh Hour*, *Casablanca: The Poem*, and *Casanova in Venice*. He typically wrote in rhyme using eleven-syllable lines, so I have adopted that form for my tribute to him."

BRECKEN HANCOCK's poems have appeared or are forthcoming in *Best American Experimental Writing*, *Papirmass*, *Lemon Hound*, *The Globe and Mail*, and *Hazlitt*. Her first book, *Broom Broom* (Coach House, 2014), was named by *The Globe and Mail*'s Jared Bland as a debut of the year and appeared on a number of year-end best-book lists, including the *National Post*, All Lit Up, and BookThug's Best Reads. She lives in Ottawa.

Of "Evil Brecken," Brecken writes, "Self-hatred is a difficult subject to tackle. It's easy to fall into pathos, false modesty, a pose—too often the urge to articulate one's flaws comes from a desire to be placated by the listener, to hear *no, you're not horrible… you're beautiful, brilliant, beloved*. In order to write the poem, I would need to get beyond the desire for prettification; I would need to vilify myself microscopically. There would be no room for counter-argument. It required brutal evisceration—the effort dredged up a devastating awareness of my physical and psychic ugliness and the poem was agonizing to write. But before I began I also considered what might rescue the subject matter from mere exhibitionism. The palate was essential to the poem's becoming: the poem proceeded from sound. I made lists of words that started with *br*, enclosed the hard *ck* or ended with *en*. Working with the material, making disturbing anxieties come to life, fitting the rhymes and slant-rhymes together like a puzzle—this was *fun*. I became the character; I reveled in the abuse. The poem describes competing forces within the same psyche, and I found that completing the poem necessitated accessing an internal landscape where I was at once victim and villain. This is the essential paradox the poem encapsulates: the despair of self-harm coupled with the revelry of play."

LEAH HORLICK is a writer from Saskatoon. A 2012 Lambda Literary Fellow in Poetry, her work has appeared in *Grain, Plenitude, Poetry Is Dead, Lemon Hound,* and *Canadian Poetries.* Her first book of poetry, *Riot Lung* (Thistledown Press, 2012), was shortlisted for a 2013 ReLit Award and a Saskatchewan Book Award. She lives on unceded Coast Salish territories and co-curates REVERB, a queer and anti-oppressive reading series. Her most recent collection, *For Your Own Good,* was released by Caitlin Press in spring 2015.

Of "The Tower," Horlick writes, "In the symbolism of the Tarot, the Tower is one of the most fraught cards, indicating a sudden change, a flash of insight, or a disaster. This poem was one of the most difficult to complete in *For Your Own Good* because of the questions it raises about grief, change, and disaster. There are undertones of the Jewish tradition of arguing with God—*why me? why us? why did this happen?*—something that was very present for me in my trip to Europe, where I visited cities including Prague, Berlin, Vienna, Budapest, and the former concentration camp at Dachau. I am fascinated by how our bodies and hearts inherit ancestral memory, and how that inheritance can itself be a trauma, a legacy, and a form of healing. This poem is a complicated contrast of rites of passage for young women: first love, travel, and history unfolds to reveal sexual assault, loss, and genocide. But there is also the sense of possibility brought about by disaster: when the tower collapses, what might we rebuild?"

STEVIE HOWELL is the author of the Gerald Lampert Award-nominated book, *Sharps.* "Ballad of Blood Hotel" won the 2015 Confederation Poets prize from *Arc Poetry Magazine.* Her poetry and critical writing have been widely published throughout Canada, including in *The Walrus, Maisonneuve, Eighteen Bridges,* the *National Post,* and *Quill and Quire.* In addition to writing, Stevie works as a psychometrist at a hospital and studies cognitive neuropsychology. You can read more at: steviehowell.ca

Of "Ballad of Blood Hotel," Howell writes, "In my early twenties, I worked at the huge HMV on Yonge Street in Toronto, and a friend of a friend, a famous photographer in New York, extended an offer to me to work on a film about one of my favourite living artists, Bill Callahan. It was a strange undertaking on his part, since this guy dealt primarily with A-list celebs, and I had no experience in film. Maybe in part for those two reasons, the film never happened, but a lot else did. The style of the poem is an homage to Bill Callahan's aesthetic and one can only hope he never sees it."

CATHERINE HUNTER is the author of three poetry collections, including *Latent Heat* (McNally Robinson Manitoba Book of the Year, 1997), and five works of fiction. Her new novel, *After Light*, spans three generations in a story about a blinded WWII veteran and his family. She teaches at the University of Winnipeg.

Of "Disappointment," Hunter writes, "Last winter I hurt my arm and was unable to write or do most of my normal chores, including filling the bird feeder. I was looking out the window, watching the poor chickadees and sparrows return again and again to the empty feeder and felt sad, unable to help them. Last winter was extraordinarily cold, even for Manitoba, and the snow was extraordinarily high. I was remembering how my father used to warn us kids that we could literally freeze to death outside, and we would kind of shrug, being used to it, having being born into it. My parents have both died, but sometimes I dream they are alive. Once in a dream I met my mother at a bus stop. She wanted to go home, and I was trying to stop her, but I was too ashamed to admit that my brothers and I had moved all her things out of her apartment. In another dream, my father appeared in the yard of the house where we used to live (sold many years ago). He wanted me to take him inside, and I was stalling him, not wanting to tell him the truth. Maybe this poem is about guilt, never adequately being able to take care of those you love. But it is also about writing and, somehow, baking a cake. Or not baking a cake. Because you never took the time to learn how. You were writing."

AMANDA JERNIGAN is the author of two books of poems, *Groundwork*—shortlisted for the Pat Lowther Award and named a best book of the year by National Public Radio—and *All the Daylight Hours*, and of the prose-work *Living in the Orchard: The Poetry of Peter Sanger*. She edited *The Essential Richard Outram* and co-edited, with Evan Jones, *Earth and Heaven: An Anthology of Myth Poetry*. She lives in Hamilton, Ontario, with her family.

Of "Io," Jernigan writes, "In Ovid's *Metamorphoses*, Io, daughter of the river god Inachus, is raped by Zeus, who then transforms her into a white heifer—an unsuccessful attempt to hide his infidelity from his vengeful wife. Unrecognizable to her family, Io wanders the earth in this form—first captive to Argus the hundred-eyed, Hera's appointed jailer; then tormented by a Fury—until at length, beside the river Nile, she regains her natural shape. In some accounts Io's tormentor is a gadfly, but in A.D. Melville's translation of the *Metamorphoses*, the tormentor is a Fury set 'Before her... eyes and in her mind': a demon, like the marks of trauma, as much internal as external. 'Io' is one in a series of *Metamorphoses* poems—each ten lines long, in loosely-rhyming couplets—that I began writing after my first son's birth. They were poems that I could work on in my head as I was nursing a baby or pulling a wagon: formal exercises in repetition-and-variation. But at the same time, they were meditations on change, coming out of a time of life in which metamorphosis is everywhere apparent. The register of these poems is mythological, but the impetus is personal: this is true of the series as a whole, and also of the individual poems with their dramatis personae in whose stories I have seen my own both told and changed. 'Io' is for my sister."

ELENA JOHNSON's first book of poetry, *Field Notes for the Alpine Tundra* (Gaspereau Press, 2015), was written and researched during her time as writer-in-residence at a remote ecology research station in the Yukon's Ruby Range. Her poetry has been longlisted for the CBC Literary Awards and shortlisted for the Alfred G. Bailey Poetry Prize. Her work is featured in *Lemon Hound*'s New Vancouver Poets folio and has appeared in numerous journals and anthologies. elenajohnson.ca.

Of "I Don't Bother Canning Peaches," Johnson writes, "I used to can peaches, as well as tomatoes and pears. I harvested and dried herbs. I always had a garden. In recent years, I've been physically unable to tackle such things, mostly because of the bending and lifting involved. So, currently, I don't can peaches. As a result, I've been reflecting on what a privilege it is to be able to do these things—to have the time, the energy, the money to invest in supplies, the able-bodiedness, the access to land. And then I reflect on what it means to not preserve local food at all: What assumptions are we making, by not bothering to can peaches? The poem is an answer to that question. A few months after this poem was published, I was at a party, chatting with a small group of people I'd never met before. The man across from me said, "Wait—this conversation reminds me of a poem I just read." He pulled a magazine out of his bag and opened it to the appropriate page. 'It's by Elena Johnson,' he said, then paused. 'She's not here, is she?' I couldn't help laughing with surprise, so had to confess it was me. He read the poem aloud at the party—a beautiful, clear reading. It was this poem. As poets, we so rarely receive feedback from strangers who read our work. It was a comfort to me, knowing that this poem had meant something to this man, to the extent that he felt compelled to read it out loud."

TROY JOLLIMORE is a native of Nova Scotia and has lived in California since 1999. He is the author of *At Lake Scugog* and *Tom Thomson in Purgatory*, which won the 2006 National Book Critics Circle Award. He has also authored two philosophical works: *Love's Vision* and *On Loyalty*. He has received fellowships from the Bread Loaf Writers' Conference and the Guggenheim Foundation. His third book of poems, *Syllabus of Errors*, will be published by Princeton in Fall 2015.

Of "Some Men," Jollimore writes, "I heard someone tell a joke that began, 'A man walks into a bar,' and it got me thinking about jokes as a literary form, about how jokes get preserved, communicated, and performed, how they constitute a kind of oral storytelling tradition, the way—as with many types of stories—a joke consists of an essential core that is held constant, plus a surrounding field of changeable details in which improvisation is permitted, so that each telling of a joke is unique. And the way jokes evolve, and sometimes give birth to other jokes; sometimes you realize, even in the midst of telling one, that what's truly funny about the joke is not what you had thought, that there is a second, subtler, funnier joke hiding inside the first. Or that the joke's central insight is not what you at first thought. It seemed curious to me that the phrase 'A man walks into a bar' is used as a standard opening for a certain genre of joke, given so many of the things that can happen when men walk into bars are not funny at all. But of course, jokes are so often used to talk about what is sad and frightening and difficult. At any rate, I wrote the poem quickly; the only hard part was choosing the cat's name. I went through a lot of different names for the cat, even though, in retrospect, it is blazingly obvious that the cat's name is Simon."

KASIA JUNO was born in South Africa and immigrated to Canada at the age of twelve. Kasia's fiction, poetry and comics can be found in *The Rumpus*, *Maisonneuve*, *GUTS: Canadian Feminist Magazine*, *The Puritan*, and *SAND: Berlin's English Literary Journal*. In 2009, she received the Quebec Writer's Federation short story prize. Kasia is currently at work on a collection of short stories and a novel. She lives in Montreal. kasiajuno.weebly.com

Of "Lake Vostok from the Perspective of a Yeti Crab," Juno writes, "A few winters ago, I was sitting in an unheated flat in Berlin, thinking: This must be the coldest place on Earth. But when I googled 'the coldest place on Earth' it turned out to be in Antarctica, at the Vostok research station. The thing that fascinates scientists about Lake Vostok, a buried lake roughly the size of Lake Ontario, is that it is untouched, sealed off from the rest of the world for millions of years. Some believe that it contains clues to the possibility of life on other planets. It may be home to a whole new life form, to something as mysterious and resilient as the Yeti crabs, which, until very recently, were unknown to us, too. For me, this poem is about frontiers, Earth's final frontier. About what is gained as well as what is lost with human beings' need to explore, penetrate, and categorize. There are so few 'undiscovered' places on Earth; they become a canvas on which we project our fears and desires. This is my imagined Lake Vostok."

JAMES LANGER lives in St. John's. His first book, *Gun Dogs*, was published by Anansi in 2009, and he co-edited *The Breakwater Book of Contemporary Newfoundland Poetry*.

Of "St. John's Burns Down for the Umpteenth Time" Langer writes, "The city of St. John's has always had an uneasy relationship with fire and has, in fact, burned down a number of times. But this poem is an attempt to create a kind of urban pastiche, to write about the recent dislocation of the city's lower classes—which has occurred during an ongoing process of downtown gentrification—as if laid over the ghosts of two other historic events: The Great Fire of 1892 and the riot of April 1932. All cities change, and I sought to document the experiences of helplessness and defeat, the incidental damages, which arise within this system of historic (and therefore economic) cycles. Prosperity has been piped into the city like a gas, and prosperity is a good thing, but I wanted to check for leaks by lighting a match, so to speak."

CAROLE GLASSER LANGILLE is the author of four books of poems and a collection of short stories. She has been nominated for the Atlantic Poetry Prize and The Governor General's award. *Church of the Exquisite Panic: The Ophelia Poems* is her most recent book. A collection of her linked short stories will be published by Gaspereau in October 2015. She is also the author of two children's books.

Of "Left," Glasser Langille writes, "The beginning of the poem is autobiographical. I did meet Michael Gross when I was fifteen and in summer camp. He was very sick that summer. Over the next four decades we remained friends and kept in touch sporadically. Then he wrote to tell me he had ALS. I tried to capture his kindness in the poem: 'he waited hours in a blizzard for my plane/ when I visited.' My old dog was with me when I read the news about Michael, and followed me up and down stairs. I repeated the dog and plum and stair imagery in the latter lines so the poem would be cohesive. Regarding the line, 'When we kissed I thought, *here's a place to be admitted*,' I met Michael when I was young. Romance between young people does seem to be about being 'admitted' to that rarified society of coupledom, something that seemed so out of reach, at least for me, when I was a teen. The line 'The body is an alibi when the mind roams,' just came to me and is one of the gifts one gets when involved in the inner life of a poem. Michael was very generous. Though he is no longer alive, I like to think he is still assisting me and perhaps it is because of him that the poem was chosen for your anthology."

JEFF LATOSIK lives in Toronto and published *Safely Home Pacific Western* in the spring of 2015 with the Icehouse Imprint of Goose Lane editions. He is the author of *Tiny, Frantic, Stronger* (2010). His work has appeared in magazines and journals across the country and won the Trillium Book Award for Poetry in 2011.

Latosik writes, "'Safely Home Pacific Western' is a short tongue-in-cheek journey. It's an odd personal journey, but it's also about our collective journey through those 'demotions' Carl Sagan coined. Sagan framed these in terms of the universe (insular geocentrism giving way to humbling heliocentrism, for example); SHPW frames them in terms of the 'inward turn' of conscious experience present explicitly and implicitly in poetry and everywhere in our day-to-day lives. Confusions abound: how that turn seems already co-opted and consolidated from the get-go; how it seems influenced by elements beyond our control (no sense of the 'homely' here); how science keeps pulling us away from a 'common-sensical' notion of what consciousness and interiority are; and how—despite the failures we've known about since at least Nietzsche—there is a way in which inward journeys seem so stubbornly to swerve towards pattern-seeking, to gesture towards some sense of a universal, to be human in short. Is it really a matter of just sloughing off this feature of our experience, of steadfastly denying the appearances that interiority affords us, or does the problem run deeper than that? The poem tries to follow that question down a rabbit hole."

TANIS MACDONALD is from Winnipeg but has lived in Waterloo, Ontario since 2006. She is the author of three books of poetry, including *Rue The Day* (Turnstone Press), and her poetry has appeared in *The New Quarterly*, *Contemporary Verse 2*, *Poetry is Dead*, *Prairie Fire*, among others. She teaches Canadian literature and creative writing at Wilfrid Laurier University.

Of "Small Fierce Fact," MacDonald writes, "I have been turning over the questions of infertility and adoption in my mind for a while, and in 'Small Fierce Fact,' I was thinking about how they might have been discussed in the 1960s, before the boom in reproductive technologies. What would it be like to come from a long line of barren women? I recast the image of the chosen baby as a heroine unto herself: a daughter whose fierce sense of rebellion is part of her inheritance from her adoptive mother. Shaking the foundations of the family tree is an adoptee's job—and it's a feminist question, too, to consider how women inherit from each other despite genetics, despite patriarchy, despite capitalism."

MARCUS MCCANN is the author of two books of poems, *Soft Where* (2009) and *The Hard Return* (2012), and a dozen chapbooks, most recently *Shut Up Slow Down Let Go Breathe* (2015). He's the winner of the E.J. Pratt Medal and the John Newlove Award, and a finalist for the Gerald Lampert Award. He is a lawyer, and a part owner of Toronto's Glad Day Bookshop. marcusmccann.com.

Of "The Jeweller's Made Uncountable Examples," McCann writes, "A quirk of our digital age is the ability to photograph one's penis, if you have one, and send that photograph to others. At the risk of shocking older and younger readers, I can confirm that this happens often enough. These pictures are sometimes sent to others unsolicited, and it is this phenomenon that is the subject of 'The Jeweller's Made Uncountable Examples.' How does the narrator feel about receiving such photos? Is it the sexual content or the aesthetic quality which the narrator quarrels with? And what does the narrator mean by 'I've seen the world's one / dick pic'? Perhaps the title provides a clue: it's a line from 'A Display of Mackerel' by American poet Mark Doty, which refers to fish in a market stall as 'Splendor, and splendor, / and not a one in any way // distinguished from the other.'"

SADIE MCCARNEY grew up in New Glasgow and Annapolis Royal, Nova Scotia, and still finds herself writing her way around those landscapes. Her poetry and fiction have appeared in *Prairie Fire*, *Plenitude*, *The Puritan*, *PANK*, and magazines (such as *Room*) that don't begin with P. In 2010, Sadie received the Lieutenant Governor's Award for Artistic Achievement from the Nova Scotia Talent Trust. She has spent the last few years roaming between Nova Scotia and Prince Edward Island.

McCarney writes, "'Steeltown Songs' is a fiction, but it came to me by way of two real places: the gritty little collection of mostly-failed industrial towns called

Pictou County, Nova Scotia (where I grew up), and the heartache of a series of entirely-hopeless childhood crushes. I did most of the real writing work when I was sixteen and seventeen, but the poem had no real form then and spoke in a very distant and impersonal third-person voice. Still, I found myself drawn to the nameless lapsed-tomboy character who would later become my narrator. The day of my grade twelve prom, instead of spending hours getting my hair done for the dance, I brought a very early and incomplete draft of 'Steeltown Songs' to a poetry workshop with George Elliott Clarke. I very nervously read my fragments of poetry aloud at top speed, and everyone at the workshop encouraged me to keep working on it. But it was also hinted gently (and mercifully) that the poem wasn't quite there yet. The intervening five or six years have been mostly editing, but the process has taught me something important: never give up on a character. Never give up on a poem."

AMBER MCMILLAN is a teacher and writer, originally from Ontario, living on Protection Island, BC with her family. Her poems have appeared in Canadian magazines and journals such as *Arc*, *CV2*, *subTerrain* and others. *We Can't Ever Do This Again* (Wolsak and Wynn, 2015) is her first collection of poems.

McMillan writes, "'Listen, Junebug' is a poem for my seven-year-old daughter. This poem, more than others in the collection, most obviously lays out a major theme I was grappling with: the conflict, and ultimate resolution, of the personal experience moving outward toward some universal relevance. That is to say, how the personal, in this case the deeply intimate relationship of parent and child, can transform when widened outward, or when the barriers of intimacy are loosened. I wanted to write a poem about my daughter that wasn't about me but was about her, and moreover, about her in the world independent of me: her in the world with Fat Joe the Rapper, President Obama, and prostitution rings."

CARA-LYN MORGAN was born in the thick of winter on the Saskatchewan prairie. A seventh-generation Métis on her mother's side, and a first-generation Canadian on her Trinidadian-born father's side, her work often explores the parallels of colonialism existing between these distinct cultures. She graduated from the University of Victoria's Creative Writing Program, and currently lives in the Toronto area. Her debut collection, *What Became My Grieving Ceremony*, was released in 2012.

Of "mîscacakânis," Morgan writes, "This poem is about reconnecting with the ancestral instinct, the ghost bones, and the places in the earth where the old family has always walked. It is about relearning the joy of space and distance; unfamiliar to those of us who have always lived surrounded in the concrete and shade of cities. My body always knows when it is back on the prairies, there is a lightening in my shoulders and my feet seem to soften. When my baby niece came to Watrous from Toronto, she seemed to feel this loosening even though she had never been to Saskatchewan before. She ran ahead of us, screaming joyfully with her hands flung up above her head. In that moment, I realized that the span of prairie is not a thing that can be described or learned; it is a nesting in the chest, a way of breathing. It is something that our oldest bones understand. This is also a poem about the sharing of stories, the rooting back to the familial voices, and the act of coming home. It was written in couplets not only to echo the pairing of the speaker and the child she is observing, but also to create expanse on the page using long lines and a lot of white space. The poem is meant to be visually wide as well as visceral, through the use of adjectives and sensory language, to loosely echo the stretch of the prairie horizon, its sharp edge and widest skies."

A.F. MORITZ's most recent book is a long poem, *Sequence* (House of Anansi Press). His poetry has received various notices, including the Award in Literature of the American Academy of Arts and Letters, the Guggenheim Fellowship, the Griffin Poetry Prize, the Bess Hokin Prize of *Poetry* magazine, the Ingram Merrill Fellowship, the ReLit Award, and the Raymond Souster Award of the League of Canadian Poets; three of his books have been finalists for the Governor General's Award.

Of "Entrances," Moritz writes, "A long time ago I was deeply moved by Georg Trakl's lines in 'De Profundis' where it says, 'The silence of God / I drank from the spring in the forest'. For me this correlates with Hopkins, '…nature is never spent; / There lives the dearest freshness deep down things'. Similar is the realization that dawns on you in reading Paz, that 'nature' can be pushed away but only to the point of its absolute persistence in the form of night, the empty plenitude, whatever lies beneath and fountains forth. The realization that that is what Paz ultimately means by nature. Everything else can be destroyed, I suppose, or at least traduced, but this persists. We tend to think it persists as the unavoidable end, but it persists as the field of possibility and as possibility itself. Reading 'Entrances' now, I think this is what it's about. The impulse as in Trakl to go out from noisy humankind, always shoving at you, marching you, demanding, commanding, incessant, and find the relief of the silence of

God. In the wilderness. To find this 'beyond' in a world that people try to make have no beyond. To find this 'within' in the cracks that people can't keep from opening. To find it in night and death when it has been all but razed from life and day. I'd like the poem's title to be read also, simultaneously, with the accent on the second syllable."

SHANE NEILSON is a poet, physician, and critic from New Brunswick. His third book of poems, *On Shaving Off His Face*, was released with the Porcupine's Quill in Spring 2015. Shane was shortlisted for the Trillium Poetry Prize in 2010 and he won the Robin Blaser Award from *The Capilano Review* this year. This is his second appearance in the *Best Canadian Poetry* series.

Of "My daughter imitates A.Y. Jackson's 'Road to Baie St. Paul,'" Neilson writes, "About a year after my daughter and son were seriously ill, but somewhat on the way to recovery, my daughter, Zee, came home from school with a painting. As part of a grade eight art class, she imitated the A.Y. Jackson painting mentioned in the poem's title. After handing the portrait to me, she asked, 'What do you think, Daddy?' I'm sure I praised her, but my reaction is subsumed in the more serious reaction that is the poem I wrote about an hour after she asked me that originating question. In her painting, I saw a speck of a man hurtling home on a horse and carriage, desperate to find his family intact. The man had a sick daughter, sick son, and a heart as vacant as the depicted landscape was violent. The horseman saw angels, and he knew he had to hurry. The place was too beautiful for him not to be worried. The man in the painting—he wrote my poem. When I learned the bargain fathers and mothers make with life, that it is fleeting, that there is no guarantee the things we love will stay, but that we are yet impotently alive to mark their passing, I reached for several texts to assist with the absorption of this truth of impermanence. One of them is William James, who appeared to me as one of the angels who said, 'The beautiful polices the most solemn passions.' I worked on that poem until it was as solemn as I could make it sound, to follow James' advice, to make the poem grieve."

HOA NGUYEN is the author of four full-length collections of poetry, including *As Long As Trees Last* (Wave, 2012) and *Red Juice, Poems 1998–2008* (Wave, 2014). Born in the Mekong Delta, Nguyen currently lives in Toronto where she curates a reading series and teaches poetics privately and at Ryerson University.

Nguyen writes, "The title of the poem 'A Thousand Times You Lose Your Treasure' is also the working title of a series in-progress, a verse meditation on a convulsive era in Vietnam. In this poem as in others in the series, I'm presenting and reimagining personal, historical, and familial perspectives."

ALEXANDRA OLIVER was born in Vancouver and currently lives just outside of Toronto. Her most recent book, *Meeting the Tormentors in Safeway* (Biblioasis, 2013), was named a Canadian Poetry Book of the Year by *The National Post* and won the Pat Lowther Memorial Award. Oliver is the co-editor (with Annie Finch) of *Measure for Measure: An Anthology of Poetic Meters* (Random House/ Everyman, 2013.) She also writes about film.

Oliver writes, "I wrote 'Margaret Rose' because, as a (rather awkward) child, I had always been fascinated by Princess Margaret. On the most basic level, her beauty went beyond aristocratic elegance; it was sensual, feline. The vibe she gave off was sex, sex, sex, even if (at ten) I didn't really know what that was. There was also the factor of her reputation. She was painted as a snob, a Jezebel and a boozehound. She was highly intelligent, but notoriously unpredictable. And, all the while, there was the Queen, forging ahead impassively, like a pillbox-hatted war machine. Margaret didn't have a chance. There's that famous exchange with Gore Vidal, when she told him, 'It was inevitable: when there are two sisters and one is the Queen, who must be the source of honour and all that is good, the other must be the focus of the most creative malice, the evil sister.' Two women, one with power invested in her, the other with an 'evil' animal power that could only embarrass and destroy. Margaret was ground down and eliminated, not by her own appetites, but by the fact that she was the foil to an untarnishable emblem. As flawed as she was, I found her sort of heroic. Today I still feel floppy, messy, unfinished, and yet the appetites (often for all the wrong things) never die. I wanted to write a hymn to the joy of living, of failing, in (paradoxically) as mannered a form as possible."

MICHAEL PACEY lives and writes in his hometown of Fredericton, NB. His poems have appeared in a number of Canadian literary magazines, including *The New Quarterly*, *The Fiddlehead*, *Exile*, *Prairie Fire*, *The Malahat Review* and *The Dalhousie Review*. Signature Editions published a full-length collection, *The First Step*, in 2011. These poems are included in *Electric Affinities*, published in the spring of 2015, also from Signature. He is currently working on a collection of poems inspired by HD Thoreau's Journal, tentatively titled *Nature is My Bride*.

Pacey writes, "The idea for the poem 'Lightbulb' came to me like, well, a lightbulb. A switch was thrown in my mind. I'm drawn to everyday objects which possess an iconic or symbolic status, and I knew that the lightbulb, with all its secondary denotations of idea and intellectual discovery, would prove to be a rewarding subject. I began to brainstorm, trying to find all associations and connotations connected to lightbulbs in my memory-bank. First of all, I retrieved images of my father performing various chores in the light of a naked bulb. Then I mused on my subject in the marketplace, from a consumer's perspective: the business of choosing shade and wattage, and how it feels to walk out of the store with a product in your bag that seems to amount to nothing. Then it struck me how the bulb is often used to represent the opposite of intellectual acuity, as in all those 'lightbulb jokes' that begin, 'How many blanks does it take to screw in a lightbulb?'—as if this task of installation is the nadir of functioning intelligence. The act of purchase is followed by the return home, and the subsequent realization of to what extent our modern concept of domicile is dependent upon incandescent illumination. The penultimate stanza, my favourite section, came in a brainwave: I realized my most memorable encounter with lightbulbs occurred when I had left one on overnight, and the guilt I felt that it had been up all that time, while I slept unaware. Appropriately, the conclusion of the poem deals with the death of the lightbulb: the noise it makes when it gives out, gives up, the noise it makes when you give it a final shake. The poem conflates the electric activity of the light bulb with the electric activity of our thoughts, the electric nature of the human brain."

SARA PETERS was born in Antigonish, NS. She was a 2010-2012 Stegner fellow at Stanford, and her work has appeared in *Poetry* magazine, *The Threepenny Review*, *The Walrus*, *Slate*, and *Poetry Wales*, among other places. Her first book is *1996*.

Of "After His Brother's Body Washed Ashore, Roman," Peters writes, "1. I used to house and dog sit for my friend Sarah Frisch and her family, who lived in the Outer Mission district of San Francisco. 2. As kids, my sister Morgan and I used to do something we called 'Famous Dancing.' We also shared a bedroom for many years. 3. I was imagining a brittle, intellectually arrogant person with a contemptuous manner and a tendency toward self-punishment. I was imagining how such a person might cope with life-altering grief. 4. I was also thinking about memories within memories, and the chambered nature of human minds, and how a person, if so inclined, could retreat endlessly into their own psyche, opening ever-smaller doors. 5. Finally: I love llamas, though their personalities are frequently shitty."

MATT RADER is the author of three collections of poetry and the story collection, *What I Want to Tell Goes Like This* (2014). Raised on the Salish Sea in unceded K'ómoks territory, Rader's work has appeared in magazines, journals, and anthologies around the world. He is a member of the core faculty in the Department of Creative Studies at the University of British Columbia Okanagan. He lives with his family in the City of Kelowna, in traditional Sylix lands.

Of "SN1987AZT," Rader writes, "According to the Okanagan Nation Alliance, Sylix is a word that takes its meaning from several different images including the braiding of fibre. In the winter of 1987 a super nova made the news. It was the first time in centuries that the phenomenon had been visible to the naked eye. That year, the man who had been acting as a nanny to me and my brothers, while my mum worked long hours in child-protection, tested positive for HIV. Before caring for us he had been a big-game guide in the Yukon, and he knew about the stars. He and I spent many hours looking at the moon and the constellations through his spotting scope. This poem is a result of the blooming confusion of memory that conflated those hours looking at the sky with news of the supernova and my first, up close, view of the terror of HIV/AIDS, a terror that, in the West, was particular to the 1980s."

KYEREN REGEHR lives in Victoria, BC, with her family. Her poetry has been published in literary journals and anthologies in Canada, Australia and America. She completed her first full-length manuscript, *Cult Life*, with the assistance of a grant from the Canada Council for the Arts, and gratefully received a second Canada Council grant in 2015 to work on her new collection. "Dorm Room 214" received an honourable mention in *The Fiddlehead's* 2014 poetry contest.

Regehr writes, "'Dorm Room 214' emerged during my MFA. My thesis manuscript was based on the years I'd spent in a rather cultish ashram, and as I began to dig into the past the writing became an exorcism of sorts. Much of the poetry emerged in prose form—it was as if it resisted lineation because breaks might halt or hiccup the monologue-style flow. Listening to the rhythms and internal rhyme was a priority—there are a lot of different thoughts on what prose poetry is and can be, and at the time I felt it required a condensed and musical voice, so I tried to be true to that. A persona for the manuscript began to emerge with this poem, a quasi-me who became representative of the ashram as a whole and the kind of lackadaisical spirituality practiced there. I began playing with composite characters, but blending two or more real-life people into a sort of literary distillation of the truth was complicated territory. Was I simply hiding behind the changes I had made (the life I wrote about was no longer wholly mine)? How would the other 'characters' feel if they read the work? Facts were kept/discarded/altered for all sorts of poetic and personal reasons. In the end I tried to present an emotionally accurate depiction of the way things were, but how much can the truth be 'crafted' without losing its essence? It's wobbly ground."

BRENDA SCHMIDT lives in Creighton, a mining town on the Canadian Shield in northern Saskatchewan. She is the author of four books of poetry and a book of essays. Both her poetry and nonfiction have been shortlisted for Saskatchewan Book Awards. She is a past winner of the Alfred G. Bailey Prize and was shortlisted for the CBC Literary Award for Poetry several times.

Of "A Citizen Scientist's Life Cycle," Schmidt writes, "The epigraph for this poem comes from one of the interviews I conducted for *Culvert Installations*, a book project in progress wherein I consider the way stories emerge and flow. Basically I go through the words I'm given and respond in some way. In this case, the word 'mean' reminded me of a sonnet I'd written after I'd completed a bird survey a few years before. The survey was one of many citizen science projects I've taken part in over the years, though always with a certain uneasiness. The hat of the naturalist has never fit comfortably. There are a number of culverts along the route and I stop near the same ones year after year to search for certain species. This process of returning and searching and the strict constraints of the surveys frequently lead me to the sonnet form, a place where I can argue and tromp around and not scare anything. Sometimes I flush out something new to me, something I hadn't considered before. Naturally the epigraph brought to mind, too, the cycle of seasons and the seasons of life and soon I found myself writing a sonnet cycle using my mean old sonnet as a way in."

MELANIE SIEBERT's first poetry collection, *Deepwater Vee* (McClelland & Stewart), was a finalist for Canada's Governor General's Literary Award. Melanie completed an MFA at the University of Victoria where she received the Lieutenant Governor's Silver Medal for her master's thesis. She has worked for many years as a wilderness guide on rivers in the Northwest Territories, Nunavut, and Alaska.

Siebert writes, "'Thereafter' riffs on and raids from 'Which Way Madness Lies,' by Rachel Aviv (*Harper's*, December 2010), and 'They Shoot Buffalo, Don't They,' by Christopher Ketcham (*Harper's*, June 2008). Aviv reports on the prodromal phase that precedes a psychotic break with reality, while Ketcham's piece describes horsemen and helicopters hazing bison in an attempt to keep them in the confines of a national park. The images of panicked bison pounding through sagebrush made me think of how I grew up on the prairies without any knowledge of or feel for the great herds. I was trying to sit with the fact of settlers, my forbearers, slaughtering over fifty million bison on the Great Plains, nearly driving them to extinction, making big bucks (fashion, drivebelts, etc), but also intentionally, brutally starving out Indigenous peoples and overtaking their homelands. As Rae Armantrout said of this poem, 'The word "thereafter" sits at the start like a poison pill, so full of faux inevitability it's bound to make us suspicious.' The legacy of colonization continues with the fanatical false logic of progress, with broken treaties, resource extraction and unrelenting pollution. I was wondering about the cultural and personal capacity to comprehend and absorb devastation. The poem strains to put words to ecological and psychological symptoms that to me feel common and yet also amorphous, delusional and unsayable. It's as if the soundtrack of the Real is perpetually mismatched to the way our lips are moving. Comprehension often remains just out of reach, even as we're implicated, unhinged."

BARDIA SINAEE was born in Tehran, Iran and currently lives in Toronto. His poems have appeared in magazines including *Arc*, *PRISM* and *The Walrus*. His chapbook, *Blue Night Express*, is available from Anstruther Press.

Sinaee writes, "'Escape from Statuary' is a self-help poem of sorts. After reading *The Art of Recklessness*, Dean Young's book about poetry, I took to heart his message that poets should forgive themselves for not being perfect. I looked back at my own work and recognized how anxiety about whether or not I was a capital-P Poet was manifesting itself as sarcasm, self-loathing and a sense of preordained failure. 'Escape from Statuary' is my response to this realization. To write it, I indulged in the zealous proclamations most critics hate, and aimed away from the sober, agnostic poetry that vies for a place in the canon and a statue in the park. Therefore it feels delightfully ironic to see the poem anthologized."

ADAM SOL's fourth collection of poetry, *Complicity*, was published in 2014 by McClelland & Stewart, and was shortlisted for the Raymond Souster Award. His previous collections include *Crowd of Sounds*, which won Ontario's Trillium Award for Poetry in 2004; and *Jeremiah, Ohio*. He has published fiction, scholarly essays, and reviews for a variety of publications, including *PANK*, *Lemon Hound*, and *Joyland.com*. He is an associate professor at Laurentian University's campus in Barrie, Ontario, and lives in Toronto with his wife, Rabbi Yael Splansky, and their three sons.

Of "Nearly Blank Calendar," Sol writes, "My two grandmothers are total badasses—one was driving a silver convertible into her nineties, and is still making trouble at a home in Rhode Island. The other was a New Yorker whose interests and intonation are permanently inscribed on me. I don't tend to write very autobiographical poems, but I've revisited the scenes of her taking care of my grandfather at the end of his life over and over again. What struck me at the time (I was in my late teens) wasn't just the daily work of nursing him, but rather her complete nonchalance. It was hard, bitterly hard, to see her husband disappear, but she had no use for complaining. Her stoicism wasn't just dutiful; it had a lot of pride. There's also an aspect of the poem that is in conflict with itself, because a woman like this would never want the story told in 'Nearly Blank Calendar' to be the 'story of her life.' There were so many more interesting things that happened to her, and she'd be furious with me for returning to these eighteen months, which make her life seem so much less rich than it was for over ninety years. But that's how it always is—the stories we tell, even about those we love, are reductive, and not necessarily the ones they'd want us to tell about them. In this case, I at least gave her a chance to argue with me about it. The poem was also informed by a great conversation I had with Dr. Adrian Grek, from the Reitman Centre for Alzheimer's Support, which helped give context and background. Some of the well-meaning pamphlet language came from there."

KAREN SOLIE was born in Moose Jaw and grew up in rural southwest Saskatchewan. Her most recent collection, *The Road In Is Not the Same Road Out*, was published this year in Canada by House of Anansi Press and in the U.S. by Farrar, Straus, and Giroux. A volume of selected poems, *The Living Option*, was published in the U.K. by Bloodaxe Books in 2013. She's worked for creative writing departments at York University, the University of Toronto, University of Guelph, and the University of British Columbia, and is an associate director for the Banff Centre's Writing Studio.

Of "For the Ski Jump at Canada Olympic Park, Calgary," Solie writes, "Finnish ski jumper Matti Nykänen won three gold medals in Calgary in 1988, but went on to infamy for a lifestyle that degenerated into substance abuse, reality television, violence, phone line sex work, pop music, falling asleep at the wheel and driving off bridges, and what the *Guardian* described in 2010 as a 'look of rampaging bewilderment.' Nevertheless, he remains one of Finland's most-loved celebrities. The Calgary Olympic ski jump was also the launch pad for England's Eddie 'The Eagle' Edwards, who finished last in the seventy and ninety-metre events and became the international face of the underdog. He's doing well. The ninety-metre tower is no longer usable, so steep and fast that anyone with today's gear would land on the flat ground beyond the runout and die."

ANNE MARIE TODKILL is a poet and essayist whose work has appeared in *Arc Poetry Magazine, Canadian Notes and Queries, CV2, Literary Review of Canada, The Malahat Review, The Winnipeg Review, The New Quarterly* and *Prairie Fire.* "Strontium-90" received *Arc's* Diana Brebner Prize in 2014.

Of "Strontium-90," Todkill writes, "This poem was a product of distraction, not to mention procrastination, when I was struggling to copy edit a scholarly book that was as dry as it was weighty. In the course of some fact-checking I got side-tracked by a reference to the St. Louis Baby Tooth Survey. This study (of which there have been various offshoots, including in Canada) was started in Missouri in 1958 by scientists, professionals and members of the public who were worried about the effects of radioactive fallout from nuclear test blasts. Some 300,000 teeth were collected and sent for analysis for strontium-90, a radioisotope with an affinity for bone. The results helped convince John F. Kennedy to sign the Test Ban Treaty of 1963. I'd never heard of this early example of citizen science, and it intrigued me. But why a poem? Perhaps because science and poetry can complement one another in their valuing of truth. Our environment is in our blood, our bones. The citizen scientist is saying: I am here, in a place, in a time. This is what I see. This is the world that makes me. I care about it, and I cannot extricate myself. The poet says these things, too. In these days of mobile apps, citizen science has become more nerdy, more commonplace, and possibly more powerful, giving us dynamic views of migrations, species loss, and other indicators of the state of things. In defence against the grand machinery of the world, the concerned citizen holds up tiny facts: what more poignant instance of this can there be than the offering of a child's tooth? One commentator has said the poem is a tad didactic. I don't deny it."

PRISCILA UPPAL is an internationally acclaimed Toronto poet, fiction writer, memoirist, playwright, and Professor at York University. Publications include the poetry collections *Sabotage, Traumatology,* and *Ontological Necessities* (Griffin Poetry Prize finalist); novels *The Divine Economy of Salvation* and *To Whom It May Concern*; memoir *Projection: Encounters with My Runaway Mother* (Hilary Weston

Prize and Governor General's Award finalist); and short stories *Cover Before Striking*. *Time Out London* dubbed her "Canada's coolest poet." priscilauppal.ca

Of "To My Suicidal Husband," Uppal writes, "My friend, an internationally renowned biographer, is writing a history of suicide. Her husband killed himself. We met while performing at the Sri Lankan Galle Literary Festival. I was nervous because I had left my husband alone at home when he was still struggling with a critical depression that began after his job was cut during the economic recession. He had attempted suicide earlier in the year and was still at risk. We talked about how one of the worst side-effects is how the sufferer believes their loved ones would be better off without them. My husband believed this. My friend also talked about how people would assume she had an unhappy marriage. This was far from the case. Her husband, like mine, and apparently like most men (research reveals a strong gender division here), was depressed due to work-related stresses. My husband and I had always shared our worlds fully (physical, emotional, intellectual, creative), but depression barred him from mine and I felt barred from his. I worry about how often suicide is represented in art as a romantic option to the distress of living: the beauty of Ophelia floating down a river on the ripples of verse or Anna Karenina disappearing under the train through lines of luminous prose; and how many poets my husband and I admire—Paul Celan, Sylvia Plath, Anne Sexton, Marina Tsvetaeva–ended their own lives. I wanted my husband to know I would never think of his death as beautiful. Only his life is beautiful. And I want to live it with him.""

CATRIONA WRIGHT is a writer, editor, and teacher. Her short stories and poems have appeared in *Lemon Hound*, *The New Quarterly*, *Joyland*, *Prairie Fire*, *PRISM International*, *Riddle Fence*, *Grain*, and others. In 2014, a selection of her poems won *Matrix Magazine*'s LitPop Award. She is an associate poetry editor for *The Puritan*, and her debut collection is forthcoming from Signal Editions in Spring 2017.

Of "Kiviak, or, Delicacy in Greenland," Wright writes, "I first learned about kiviak from *Human Planet*, a BBC documentary series that investigates how humans have adapted to live and thrive in harsh environments. This particular episode concerned Arctic inhabitants. Because it is often difficult for people in these regions to get enough plant-based food in their diet, they rely on mammal, fish, and bird organs for essential minerals and vitamins. I was intrigued by how this very pragmatic need had developed into kiviak, which is considered a delicacy both because its preparation is painstaking and because it is eaten at ritual events such as weddings and birthdays. Fermentation—the process that creates kiviak—is a demonic transformation, a productive rot that extends a food's life and that sometimes makes it even more nutritious than the original, or raw, ingredient. I liked how revolting fermented delicacies can seem to people who are unfamiliar with them. Blue cheese does not taste as scrumptious if you focus too long on the sapphire veins of mould, and when enjoying a Polish meal, it is best not to picture the bacteria orgies in your sauerkraut. Because I wanted to highlight and celebrate the uncanny nature of fermentation, I chose a food I suspected would be new to many people. Over the course of several drafts, I began to draw connections between kiviak and other spooky and splendid transformations and their attendant rituals: pregnancy, childbirth, and marriage."

JAN ZWICKY has published nine collections of poetry, including *Songs for Relinquishing the Earth*, which won the Governor General's Award, and, most recently, *Forge*. Her books of philosophy include *Lyric Philosophy, Wisdom & Metaphor*, and *Alkibiades' Love*, published in 2015 by McGill-Queen's. Zwicky grew up on the prairies, was educated at the universities of Calgary and Toronto, and currently lives on the west coast of Canada.

Zwicky writes, "'Depth' is from a manuscript called *The Long Walk*. It is a dark poem and a dark manuscript. The world is in a state of ecological collapse and most human societies are in a state of cultural collapse. These two facts are connected through their shared root in the technocratic juggernaut that sprang from the European Enlightenment. That juggernaut regards all beings as resources; it imagines the good life in terms of the accumulation of resources or their abstraction, money. It is a grave moral error for someone like myself—a woman whose cultural freedom is also directly connected to the Enlightenment, and who has enough access to resources to keep a roof over her head and food on the table—to imagine she is not complicit. I have not been able to figure out a satisfactory way to extract myself from involvement, but I try to bear witness."

Selected by the editors
(*in alphabetical order by author's name*)

The Antigonish Review. PO Box 5000, Antigonish, NS B2G 2W5.
  antigonishreview.com

Arc Poetry Magazine. PO Box 81060, Ottawa, ON K1P 1B1. arcpoetry.ca

Ascent Aspirations. ascentaspirations.ca

B After C. 260 Ryding Ave. Toronto, ON M6N 1H5

Border Crossings. 500–70 Arthur St., Winnipeg, MB R3B 1G7.
  bordercrossingsmag.com

boulderpavement. boulderpavement.ca

Branch Magazine. branchmagazine.com

Brick. PO Box 609, Stn. P, Toronto, ON M5S 2Y4. brickmag.com

Canadian Literature. University of British Columbia, Anthropology &
  Sociology Building, 8-6303 N.W. Marine Drive, Vancouver, BC
  V6T 1Z1. canlit.ca

Canadian Notes & Queries. PO Box 92, Emeryville, ON N0R 1A0.
  notesandqueries.ca

Canadian Poetries. canadianpoetries.com

The Capilano Review. 2055 Purcell Way, North Vancouver, BC V7J 3H5.
  thecapilanoreview.ca

Carousel. UC 274, University of Guelph, Guelph, ON N1G 2W1.
  carouselmagazine.ca

Canadian Broadcasting Corporation CBC Poetry Prize finalists. cbc.ca

Contemporary Verse 2 (CV2). 502-100 Arthur St. Winnipeg, MB R3B 1H3.
  contemporaryverse2.ca

Cordite. (Canada issue jointly edited with *Arc Poetry Magazine.*) cordite.org.au

The Dalhousie Review. Dalhousie University, Halifax, NS B3H 4R2.
  dalhousiereview.dal.ca

Descant. PO Box 314, Stn. P, Toronto, ON M5S 2S8. descant.ca (now defunct)

ditch. ditchpoetry.com (now defunct)

enRoute Magazine. Spafax Canada, 4200 Boul. Saint-Laurent, Ste. 707,
  Montréal, QC H2W 2R2. enroute.aircanada.com

Event. PO Box 2503, New Westminster, BC V3L 5B2. event.douglas.bc.ca

Exile Quarterly. Exile/Excelsior Publishing Inc., 134 Eastbourne Ave.,
  Toronto, ON M5P 2G6. exilequarterly.com/quarterly

Existere. Vanier College 101E, York University, 4700 Keele St. Toronto, ON
M3J 1P3. yorku.ca/existere

The Fiddlehead. Campus House, University of New Brunswick, 11 Garland
Court, PO Box 4400, Fredericton, NB E3B 5A3. thefiddlehead.ca

filling Station. PO Box 22135, Bankers Hall, Calgary, AB T2P 4J5.
fillingstation.ca

Forget Magazine. forgetmagazine.com

Freefall Magazine. 922-9 Avenue SE, Calgary, AB, T2G 0S4.
freefallmagazine.ca

Geist. Suite 210, 111 West Hastings St. Vancouver, BC V6B 1H4. geist.com

Grain. PO Box 67, Saskatoon, SK S7K 3K1. grainmagazine.ca

Hazlitt. penguinrandomhouse.ca/hazlitt

The Humber Literary Review. humberliteraryreview.com

The Impressment Gang. theimpressmentgang.com

The Leaf. PO Box 2259, Port Elgin, ON N0H 2C0.
bmtscom/~brucedale/leaf.htm

Lemon Hound. lemonhound.com

The Literary Review of Canada. 710-170 Bloor St. W. Toronto, ON M5S 1T9.
reviewcanada.ca

Maisonneuve. 4413 Ave. Harvard, Montréal, QC H4A 2W9.
maisonneuve.org.

The Malahat Review. University of Victoria, PO Box 1700, Stn. CSC,
Victoria, BC V8W 2Y2. malahatreview.ca

Maple Tree Literary Supplement. 1103-1701 Kilborn Ave., Ottawa,
ON K1H 6M8. mtls.ca

Matrix. 1400 Boulevard de Maisonneuve O. LB 658, Montréal,
QC H3G 1M8. matrixmagazine.org

The Nashwaak Review. St. Thomas University, Fredericton, NB E3B 5G3.
stu.ca/stu/about/publications/nashwaak/nashwaak.aspx

New Poetry. newpoetry.ca

The New Quarterly. St. Jerome's University, 290 Westmount Rd. N.
Waterloo, ON N2L 3G3. tnq.ca/

The Newfoundland Quarterly. newfoundlandquarterly.ca

Numéro Cinq. numerocinqmagazine.com

One Throne. onethrone.com

ottawater. ottawater.com

Our Times. 407-15 Gervais Dr. Toronto, ON M3C 1Y8. ourtimes.ca

(parenthetical). wordsonpagespress.com/parenthetical

Poetry Is Dead. 5020 Frances St. Burnaby, BC V5B 1T3. poetryisdead.ca

Prairie Fire. 423-100 Arthur St. Winnipeg, MB R3B 1H3. prairiefire.ca

PRISM International. Creative Writing Program, University of British Columbia, Buchanan Room E462, 1866 Main Mall, Vancouver, BC V6T 1Z1. prism.arts.ubc.ca

Pulp Literature. pulpliterature.com

The Puritan. puritan-magazine.com

Queen's Quarterly. Queen's University, 144 Barrie St. Kingston, ON K7L 3N6. queensu.ca/quarterly/

Rampike. English Dept., University of Windsor, 401 Sunset Ave. Windsor, ON N9B 3P4. uwindsor.ca/rampike

Ricepaper. PO Box 74174, Hillcrest RPO, Vancouver, BC V5V 5L8. ricepapermagazine.ca

Room. PO Box 46160, Station D, Vancouver, BC V6J 5G5. roommagazine.com

The Rotary Dial. therotarydial.ca

The Rusty Toque. therustytoque.com

17 Seconds. ottawater.com/seventeenseconds

The Steel Chisel. thesteelchisel.ca

subTerrain. PO Box 3008, MPO, Vancouver, BC V6B 3X5. subterrain.ca

Taddle Creek. PO Box 611, Station P, Toronto, ON M5S 2Y4. taddlecreekmag.com

This Magazine. 396-401 Richmond St. W. Toronto, ON M5V 3A8. this.org

The Toronto Quarterly. thetorontoquarterly.blogspot.com

Vallum. PO Box 598, Victoria Stn. Montréal, QC H3Z 2Y6. vallummag.com

The Walrus. 19 Duncan Street Ste. 101, Toronto, ON M5H 3H1. walrusmagazine.com

The Windsor Review. Department of English, University of Windsor, 401 Sunset Avenue, Windsor, ON N9B 3P4. windsorreview.wordpress.com

Untethered. alwaysuntethered.com
Zouch Magazine. zouchmagazine.com

Note: The *Best Canadian Poetry* series makes every effort to track down Canadian journals that publish poetry. The series relies on complimentary copies from the publications involved and is most grateful for the cooperation. If you are the editor or publisher of a magazine not listed and wish to be considered for future years, please add the *Best Canadian Poetry* series to your comp subscription list at the address listed in the copyright page.

"Urgent Message from the Captain of the Unicorn Hunters" appeared in *Prairie Fire* 34.4 copyright ©2014 by John Wall Barger. Reprinted with permission of the author.

"Truth, power, and the politics of Carbon Capture" appeared in *filling Station* 58 copyright ©2014 by Lesley Battler. Reprinted with permission of the author.

"Palliative Care Reflective Portfolio" appeared in *The Puritan* (Summer 2014) copyright ©2014 by Jonathan Bennett. Reprinted with permission of the author.

"The Prime Minister shook his son's hand" appeared in *The Steel Chisel* (March 2014) copyright ©2014 by Jeff Blackman. Reprinted with permission of the author.

"Two Fish" appeared in *Hazlitt* (May 26, 2014) copyright ©2014 by Julie Bruck. Reprinted with permission of the author.

"Concussed" appeared in *The Puritan* (Fall 2014) copyright ©2014 by Chad Campbell. Reprinted with permission of the author.

"The *New York Times* Uncovers Arson" appeared in *Grain* (Winter 2014) copyright ©2014 by George Elliott Clarke. Reprinted with permission of the author.

"Failed Séances for Rita MacNeil (1944-2013)" appeared in *Room* 37.2 copyright ©2014 by Lucas Crawford. Reprinted with permission of the author.

"*Ulysses*" copyright ©2014 by Robert Currie. From the collection *The Days Run Away*, published by Coteau Books, Regina, 2015. Used with permission of the publisher. "*Ulysses*" appeared in *CV2* (Fall 2014).

"That Great Burgundy-Upholstered Beacon of Dependability" from *For Your Safety Please Hold On* copyright ©2014 by Kayla Czaga, Nightwood Editions 2014, www.nightwoodeditions.com. Used with permission of the publisher. "That Great Burgundy-Upholstered Beacon of Dependability" appeared in *The Fiddlehead* (Spring 2014).

❖ EDITORS' BIOGRAPHIES ❖

Jacob McArthur Mooney's second collection, *Folk* (McClelland & Stewart, 2011), was nominated for the Trillium Book Award for Poetry and the Dylan Thomas Prize. Work from his forthcoming third collection (McClelland & Stewart, 2016) has been shortlisted for a National Magazine Award, won the *Arc* Magazine Poem of the Year and *Prairie Fire* Bliss Carman Awards, and been included in the 2012 and 2013 editions of *Best Canadian Poetry in English.* He lives with his wife and son in Toronto where he hosts and co-directs the Pivot Reading Series.

Anita Lahey is a poet, journalist, reviewer and essayist. She is the author of *The Mystery Shopping Cart: Essays on Poetry and Culture* (Palimpsest Press, 2013) and of two Véhicule Press poetry collections: *Out to Dry in Cape Breton* (2006) and *Spinning Side Kick* (2011). The former was shortlisted for the Trillium Book Award for Poetry and the Ottawa Book Award. Anita is a former editor of *Arc Poetry Magazine*, and posts occasionally on her blog, "Henrietta & Me: People and other wonders found in books." anitalahey.wordpress.com

Molly Peacock is a widely anthologized poet who writes biography, memoir, and fiction. Her newest work is *Alphabetique: 26 Characteristic Fictions*, with illustrations by Kara Kosaka. She is also the author of *The Paper Garden: Mrs. Delany Begins Her Life's Work at 72.* Her latest book of poetry is *The Second Blush* (all from McClelland & Stewart). Her poetry is the subject of Jason Guriel's monograph, *Molly Peacock: A Critical Introduction* (Story Line Press, 2014).